# SUMMARY

I0428396

In the words of Aldous Huxley:

> The charms of history and its enigmatic lessons consist in the fact that, from age to age, nothing changes and yet everything is completely different.

The same may be said of the transatlantic bargain that has underpinned the North Atlantic Treaty Organization (NATO) since its founding and framed the relationship between the United States and its European allies. A source of both enduring stability as well as perpetual discord, the transatlantic bargain has always been a balancing act between a U.S. commitment to European security in return for a position of U.S. leadership and dominance of NATO, and the expectation that Europeans would accelerate efforts to provide for their own defense. Such a balance remains the essence of the bargain in the 21st century, but the context within which the bargain must operate has changed dramatically, and the nature of America's relationship with the Alliance is perhaps under more scrutiny than ever before.

In the context of the contemporary security environment—one characterized by the complexity of modern operations requiring a range of civilian and military capabilities, and a changing world characterized by the diffusion of power and the rise of China—the Atlantic Alliance, as well as the transatlantic bargain that underpins it, must reorient itself to its changing landscape. The combined experiences of NATO's missions in the Balkans, a decade-long expeditionary operation in Afghanistan, and its most recent mission in Libya, coupled with a climate of fiscal

i

austerity on both sides of the Atlantic, have placed the bargain under immense strain. During the first Barack Obama administration, it became evident that Washington is increasingly less willing to tolerate what it sees as fundamental gaps within the Alliance—in defense spending, capabilities, and military transformation. As a result, Washington is signaling more forcefully than ever to its European allies, as well as NATO partners, that they must take on a greater share of Alliance burdens, accelerate efforts to generate capabilities and resources, and move away from a deeply entrenched culture of dependency.

Revising the bargain requires new ways of thinking, both in the United States and Europe. There are signs, however, that not only is there a consensus on the need to revise the transatlantic bargain, but that the outlines of what such a bargain might look like are beginning to emerge. U.S. rebalancing toward the Asia-Pacific and a reduction in U.S. forces in Europe in no way signal a turning away from Europe, only recognition that the United States inhabits a changing world; this is a process that essentially has been under way since the end of the Cold War, but has been accelerated in the context of the challenges and demands of a decade of war, a climate of austerity, and the rise of new centers of power. U.S. political and military leaders should continue to affirm NATO's enduring importance and value for America. The United States has already begun to signal a shift in mindset; the U.S. military is reconfiguring its force posture to reflect the wider strategic rebalancing to the Asia-Pacific, but to offset European fears over a reduced U.S. commitment to Europe, the U.S. military should, and will, continue to support regular rotational deployments to conduct joint training with its European allies and ensure both sides are able to operate together on future missions. The U.S. Army in Europe (USAREUR) will continue to play a role—albeit reduced in size—in building partner capacity and fostering interoperability through ongoing training and exercises with European allies. Continuing multinational Landpower exercises of the kind currently undertaken by USAREUR will be another valuable tool in demonstrating the U.S. military's ongoing commitment to capacity building and partnership in Europe.

At the same time, allies in Europe must learn to think about transatlantic relations with a new maturity. While Europe has its own internal difficulties that complicate the challenge of revising the transatlantic bargain at a time when multinational defense collaboration is accelerating across Europe, there are signs at least that European allies recognize and understand the importance of more efficient and coordinated efforts to generate resources and capabilities. Such efforts can play an important role in reducing their dependency on Washington.

A revised transatlantic bargain for the 21st century cannot simply be one between the United States and NATO, but must acknowledge and reflect the growing complexity of the European security architecture. Forging a truly strategic partnership among the United States, NATO, and the European Union (EU) may well require a rethinking of the relationship between these two institutions, based on a pragmatic understanding of how European security has evolved since the end of the Cold War. NATO may, at least in the short term, continue to be the primary mechanism for conducting military operations, with the EU's Common Security and Defence Policy (CSDP) playing a supporting role or assuming only small-scale missions. However, the

EU's growing competency in a range of issues from climate change and terrorism, to energy security, development, and crisis management, make the EU a critical actor in transatlantic security affairs. It must, therefore, be at the center of a revised bargain.

Such a bargain requires a shift in thinking about European security matters on both sides of the Atlantic. Washington should resist the tendency to compartmentalize the "U.S. and NATO" and the "U.S. and EU" but endeavor to encourage a more integrated and nuanced approach to transatlantic security relations. In Europe, political will and a sounder fiscal basis are required if CSDP is to achieve its potential and the EU is to take its place at the center of a revised bargain. The transatlantic bargain was a Cold War construct suited to its time; what is required now is a transatlantic bargain that can balance hope and realism, and generate a new culture of transatlantic partnership.

# A TRANSATLANTIC BARGAIN FOR THE 21ST CENTURY: THE UNITED STATES, EUROPE, AND THE TRANSATLANTIC ALLIANCE

The burdens of global citizenship continue to bind us together. A change of leadership in Washington will not lift this burden. In this new century, Americans and Europeans alike will be required to do more—not less. Partnership and cooperation among nations is not a choice; it is the one way, the only way, to protect our common security and advance our common humanity. That is why the greatest danger of all is to allow new walls to divide us from one another. The walls between old allies on either side of the Atlantic cannot stand.

Barack Obama, July 2008[1]

## INTRODUCTION

In a world characterized by flux and uncertainty, America's relationship with the North Atlantic Treaty Organization (NATO) is a constant, familiar, and reassuring presence. It is a relationship that has been at the cornerstone of U.S. national security since 1949, when the Washington Treaty brought together the United States, Canada, and 10 European nations into a formal pact, in what was a "revolutionary commitment" for a nation historically averse to "entangling alliances."[2] It is a relationship that has ebbed and flowed throughout its history, and one that has been shaped by competing impulses and dynamics. NATO has often been characterized in Washington as an Alliance beset by structural weaknesses and imbalances in burden-sharing and military capabilities, which diminish its strategic utility to the United States. Throughout its

1

lifetime, NATO has faced innumerable crises and, especially since the end of the Cold War, has been doomed to irrelevance by critics and pundits quick to write NATO's epitaph in a world far removed from the nuclear age into which it was born. For the United States in the 21st century, the Alliance seemingly has less resonance and relevance in an era defined by "failing" states, nonstate actors, amorphous terrorist and criminal networks, and the shifting dynamics of world politics. In the context of U.S. strategic rebalancing toward the Asia-Pacific, the West's economic crisis, and a decline in defense spending on both sides of the Atlantic, it would be easy to conclude that NATO is a Cold War relic that will become ever more irrelevant to U.S. strategic interests.

Such thinking is, however, a fallacy, for it obscures the very real and enduring value the Alliance continues to hold for the United States in a world in which we may be witnessing "the end of certainty."[3] NATO remains, for all its flaws, the institutional manifestation of a wider democratic security community, binding the United States to its Canadian and European allies, and a vehicle for promoting and advancing U.S. interests and values. Historically, NATO's value to the United States has been premised on the idea of a "transatlantic bargain," a concept intrinsic to an understanding of U.S.-NATO relations, past, present, and future. The term was first coined in 1970 by former U.S. Ambassador to NATO Harlan Cleveland, who spoke of a:

> glue that has held the allies more or less together . . . a large, complex, and dynamic bargain — partly an understanding among the Europeans, but mostly a deal between them and the United States of America.[4]

This deal was the result of an "invitation" from Western Europe to join a formal alliance that reflected European fears and insecurities in the face of the growing Soviet threat.[5] Accepting such an "invitation" was by no means ensured for Washington, however; the U.S. Senate remained wary of entering into a formal commitment and sought assurances that the Europeans would accelerate efforts at defense cooperation and integration. As a result, all signatories to the Alliance reached an agreement for "self-help and mutual aid," as expressed in Article III of the resulting Washington treaty. Such a clause reflected Washington's understanding that while the United States would act as the principal guarantor for European security, in return, America's European allies would endeavor to provide for their own defense. As Dean Acheson put it, this would ensure "that nobody is getting a meal ticket from anybody else so far as their capacity to resist is concerned."[6] Thus, the essence of the bargain was a balancing act: balancing U.S. commitments against European contributions to European defense.

During the Cold War, the United States consistently spent more on defense than did its European allies, but the U.S. commitment was rewarded with a dominant leadership role within the Alliance, typified by its occupation of the position of Supreme Allied Commander Europe (SACEUR). The bargain thus gave something to both sides: Europe was provided with a U.S. security guarantee, while the United States established a position of authority and dominance in an alliance that could serve as vehicle for advancing U.S. interests in Europe. However, in a post-Cold War world, the terms of the bargain have come under ever-closer scrutiny, as the Europeans have sought, but struggled to, balance their end of the bargain. Two decades of operational activity from Bosnia to Benghazi have exposed a growing capabilities gap between the United States and many of its allies, prompting growing consternation in Washington over perceptions of European "free-riding." The war in Afghanistan has proven an unforgiving crucible within which burden-sharing dynamics have played out, and by the time Barack Obama was elected to the White House in 2008 on a wave of hope and optimism, an air of crisis and pessimism was pervading Alliance politics. Although NATO is now preparing for its transition out of Afghanistan, the costs and consequences of a decade of war and the emergence of an "age of austerity" are casting dark shadows over the health and vitality of the Alliance in the 21st century, prompting renewed calls for a revised transatlantic bargain that can accommodate the economic and geopolitical realities of this century.

This monograph sets out to assess the current state of U.S.-NATO relations and, more specifically, the ways in which the United States can help forge a new transatlantic bargain. Given ongoing debates over the end of U.S. unipolarity and the "rise of the rest,"[7] the monograph aims to ask how important the U.S. leadership of NATO remains as a means of helping steer the Alliance through difficult times, or whether, in the light of fiscal challenges confronting both sides of the Atlantic, deeply rooted patterns of European dependency on U.S. leadership represent a fundamental threat to U.S. support for the Alliance. Finally, the monograph considers the need for a different kind of relationship between the United States and its NATO allies, one more attuned to the realities of the 21st century. It argues that a revised transatlantic bargain must seek to move the Alliance beyond an outdated Cold War model of U.S. leadership and European followership. To that end, the monograph explores the idea of a "post-American" alliance. Such an alliance does *not* mean a diminishing of America's commitment to the Alliance, but it does mean one in which America's European allies and partner nations take on ever-increasing responsibility at a time when America will have to balance its ongoing commitment to Europe with the challenges and demands of a changing world. As the United States increasingly looks to the Pacific rather than the Atlantic, and a new generation of U.S. policymakers comes to power that lacks the emotional commitment to NATO of its Cold War predecessors, putting the U.S.-NATO relationship onto a new footing will be vital for the health of the Atlantic Alliance in the years to come. Finally, this monograph argues that despite the current economic crisis afflicting the European Union (EU) and concern over the future of the Common Security and Defense Policy (CSDP), any revised transatlantic bargain must, by necessity, take into account the growing role and power of the EU as a global actor, and work to forge a more effective U.S.-EU-NATO partnership.

## SCOPE AND STRUCTURE

Part I aims to establish the importance of the transatlantic bargain as a means for thinking about the transatlantic Alliance, and to distill enduring themes and issues that are central to understanding U.S.-NATO relations. In particular, it explores the George W. Bush administration's relationship with the Alliance after September 11, 2001 (9/11) and the war in Afghanistan—a time when U.S.-NATO relations deteriorated sharply, generating concern on both sides of the Atlantic as to the health of the transatlantic bargain. In light of the economic crisis and the coming to power of Obama, Part II explores whether the dynamics of U.S. leadership of NATO shifted during Obama's first term in office, and how far ongoing operational challenges in Afghanistan, defense downsizing on both sides of the Atlantic, and U.S. strategic rebalancing have further fueled the debate over the need for a revised bargain. It asks what the administration's increased emphasis on the Asia-Pacific means for transatlantic relations, and examines whether NATO's operation in Libya appears to portend something of a shift in U.S. leadership of the Alliance, with the United States moving to a more supporting or enabling role for smaller-scale operations in which core U.S. interests are not at stake.

Finally, Part III aims to distill what the terms of a revised transatlantic bargain should look like, and whether a move toward a "post-American" alliance is both viable and likely, and what the implications of this may be for the United States and for the military—as well as for NATO. Part IV offers conclusions and recommendations.

## PART I. DYNAMICS OF THE TRANSATLANTIC BARGAIN

In July 2008, Democratic presidential candidate Obama visited Berlin, Germany, and in a speech that reached a global audience of millions, pledged to revitalize the transatlantic relationship that had underpinned U.S. foreign policy since 1945. His remarks came at a time when, yet again, an air of "crisis" and

6

pessimism pervaded the wider discourse on NATO and the future of transatlantic relations. Just 5 months earlier, in February 2008, U.S. Undersecretary of State R. Nicholas Burns had claimed the Alliance was facing an "existential crisis" in Afghanistan;[8] in the same month U.S. Secretary of Defense Robert Gates warned NATO was becoming a "two-tier" Alliance characterized by "some allies willing to fight and die to protect people's security, and others who are not."[9] Concern was mounting, particularly within Washington, that structural weaknesses and imbalances within the Alliance were impeding operational efficacy in Afghanistan. Commander of the International Security Assistance Force (ISAF) General James Jones declared in 2005 that national restrictions and caveats on troop deployment among some European allies had reached the "theater of the absurd."[10]

Such debates were nothing new to Alliance politics. The burden-sharing issues that are today all too familiar in Alliance discourse were established early on in NATO's history, as a result of the transatlantic bargain that was central in framing relations between the United States and its European allies. As noted in the introduction of this study, the essence of the bargain was a balancing act between the United States and Europe — the United States committing to provide a security guarantee for Europe and, in return, being rewarded with a dominant leadership position within the Alliance, while Europe was expected to accelerate efforts to provide for its own defense. Yet, much of the bargain was implicit, rather than explicit, resting on shared understandings and assumptions between the United States and its allies. As a report by the Carnegie Endowment for International Peace observes, "Each side of the Atlantic had different expectations about how interests, values, and obligations related to each other." Where Washington viewed the bargain as a "contract" implying something in return, many European countries tended to view it in less rigid terms, as a "compact" that did not necessarily translate into specific commitments.[11]

As early as 1954, U.S. frustrations with what it perceived as unequal burden sharing were evident; following the European failure to meet force goals agreed upon at the Lisbon summit, President Dwight Eisenhower bemoaned:

> I get weary of the European habit of taking our money, resenting any slight hint as to what they should do, and then assuming, in addition, full right to criticize us as bitterly as they may desire.[12]

In its role as the principal guarantor for European security, the United States has not only maintained a large U.S. military presence in Europe, but has also consistently spent more on defense as a percentage of gross domestic product (GDP) than its NATO allies, fueling notions of "unfairness" in the burden-sharing debate.[13] Still, despite persistent congressional scrutiny of Alliance burden sharing and calls for reductions in the U.S. force presence in Europe, Washington tolerated such "unfairness" partly because the bargain was also premised on a large degree of self-interest for Washington.

Both during the Cold War and in the post-Cold War years, NATO has had an enduring value to Washington as an indispensable mechanism for promoting and securing its strategic interests in Europe. In addition, the bargain lay at the heart of a wider "Atlantic Community," a term first given expression by NATO in 1956, when the report of the Committee of Three on Non-Military Cooperation recognized that the founding of NATO reflected not only the immediate threat posed by the Soviet Union, but also a growing sense of an Atlantic Community.[14] The political scientist Karl Deutsch gave further expression to this in 1957 when he spoke of NATO as an "Atlantic security community," characterized by "binding forces" within the Alliance and possibilities for cooperation beyond the realm of military security.[15]

Thus, while tensions and disputes did arise over burden sharing through the Cold War, the underlying sense of values and shared identity that bound members together helped to ensure such disagreements did not lead to any fundamental or irreparable ruptures within the Alliance. Indeed, the "community" provided the wider context within which the bargain evolved. As Karl-Heinz Kamp and Kurt Volker note, the bargain was never officially codified as a transactional *quid pro quo* arrangement; rather, it was premised on "a set of unwritten rules that were based on shared interests, values and expectations." What mattered, however, was the way in which these "unwritten rules" were interpreted over time, for "each side of the Atlantic had different expectations about how interests, values and obligations related to each other."[16] Thus, the bargain is perhaps best understood as one based on "bargaining, calculation, and a combination of shared and dissimilar values," in which the United States was the dominant power.[17] Still, the end of the Cold War injected a new dimension into the bargain: gone was the existential threat facing the Alliance, and thus the very reason that the Americans had been "invited" to provide a European security guarantee.

Some saw NATO's preservation as a reflection of America's ongoing self-interest, with the Alliance viewed as little more than "the instrument for maintaining America's domination of the foreign and military policies of the European states."[18] Others emphasized that NATO provided the United States with an existing security architecture that could serve as a mechanism for promoting stability across the Euro-Atlantic zone, and that the degree of cooperation and integration among Alliance members generated an "institutional logic" to NATO's preservation—one that served well the interests of its hegemonic state.[19] In addition, although U.S. troop numbers in Europe did decline after the end of the Cold War,[20] this was not accompanied by a more fundamental review of Alliance burden sharing, partly because of the high transactional costs involved. Washington was concerned that a "review of this particular 'burden-sharing bargain' might lead to unravelling rather than reallocation."[21]

Importantly, the nature of the burden-sharing debate also began to shift. As Jens Ringsmose notes, during the Cold War the emphasis was on inputs, with burden sharing measured in terms of the percentage of GDP spent on defense. The transition to a post-Cold War security environment, however, necessitated a rethinking of how burden sharing was measured, prompting a greater emphasis on inputs, rather than outputs, and on *how* money was spent.[22] This rethinking was premised on the belief that NATO had evolved into a wider collective-security institution committed to crisis management, in which member states were taking on a range of tasks and responsibilities. The comprehensive nature of modern military operations required a greater emphasis on contributions to the civilian dimension of operations, such as policing and economic reconstruction. Although the United States dominated many aspects of NATO's operation in Kosovo,[23] Operation ALLIED FORCE (OAF), a U.S. Department of Defense (DoD) report noted that the 13 other NATO allies that contributed to OAF provided:

> virtually all the basing facilities, air traffic coordination, and supporting elements to keep [the] air armada of over 1,000 aircraft functioning throughout the conflict.[24]

According to James Sperling and Mark Webber, European members of NATO contributed 88 percent of KFOR [Kosovo Forces] forces, while the United States contributed less than 12 percent. The NATO extraction force in Macedonia was also largely European in personnel, and remained so once deployed as KFOR in Kosovo.

Still, a perception existed in many quarters that European members of NATO were too dependent on U.S. leadership and military capabilities. It was NATO's Balkans missions that gave added impetus to European intensions to accelerate efforts to provide for their own defense, initially through the European Security and Defense Identity (ESDI). Theoretically, such a process might have allowed for the reconfiguring of the transatlantic bargain, generating a more coherent and capable Europe willing and able to take responsibility for its own security. This was wishful thinking, however. Not only was ESDI undermined by divergent intra-European perspectives on how far and fast such a process should develop, but the United States also sought to maintain the dominant position and influence the bargain had given it within Europe, and, as a result, was often openly hostile and suspicious toward ESDI. Thus, while the United States sought to promote and encourage European defense transformation, it aimed to do so through NATO and measures such as the 1999 Defense Capabilities Initiative (DCI), which sought to improve and enhance European capabilities in a number of areas. Limited progress was made in meeting the goals of the DCI, however, and by the end of the 1990s, concern was mounting in Washington as to the nature and pace of European military transformation.

Such concerns had a direct impact on U.S. attitudes to NATO in the aftermath of the 9/11 attacks on New York and Washington. After the attacks the George W. Bush administration chose to bypass the Alliance as a mechanism for conducting operations in Afghanistan, accepting contributions on a bilateral basis and seeking to pick and choose what it wanted from the Alliance collectively. Although the Alliance made some crucial contributions, notably its maritime surveillance operation in the Mediterranean, Operation ACTIVE ENDEAVOR, the perception that arose in many parts of Europe was that of an alliance snubbed by its leading member and a sense of "deflation" at the Bush administration's attitude and response.[25] Although such attitudes in part reflected the lack of expeditionary capabilities of many NATO allies, they were also indicative of a wider climate of frustration with the Alliance generated by its two Balkans campaigns. A further issue was the way in which the war on terror served to expose the contrasting lenses through which the United States and many in Europe viewed the threat from international terrorism. The events of 9/11 "brought together two parallel, yet distinct, approaches" — the United States linking Afghanistan to the wider war on terror and expansion of democracy, while many in Europe tended to view Afghanistan through the lens of state-building.[26] As Michael Williams notes:

> The allies interpreted the acts of September 11, 2001, differently, and the policies that would follow ultimately would contribute to NATO's deployment in Afghanistan and the subsequent strains the Alliance suffers today.[27]

The decision that NATO would take over command of ISAF in August 2003 appeared, initially at least, to be advantageous to both NATO and the United States. Not only did it offer NATO an opportunity to demonstrate its utility and relevance in the 21st century and move beyond the fractious disputes of the previous 2 years; this decision also served U.S. interests, given the resistance of the Bush administration to "nation-building," and provided a means by which the cost of operations could be shared—thus potentially alleviating U.S. concerns over inequitable burden sharing within the Alliance.[28] The reverse, however, proved to be true, as NATO's ISAF mission merely served to magnify existing dynamics in America's relationship with NATO, notably imbalances in burden sharing and capabilities. Moreover, as the mission in Afghanistan evolved into a broader counterinsurgency operation, so the contrasting lenses through which the United States and many of its allies viewed the conflict became ever more apparent.[29] Since the end of the Cold War, NATO had increasingly sought to remodel itself by adopting a narrative of risk management as a means of hedging against the uncertainty and unpredictability of the changed strategic landscape.[30] This was, however, an inherently problematic concept, and it was NATO's mission in Afghanistan that served to expose most forcefully the reality that, as Christopher Coker puts it, "It is in the nature of risks . . . that everything is contested—some societies take more risks than others."[31]

As noted earlier, the burden-sharing debate became more complex in the context of modern military operations; particularly in Afghanistan, it involved an increased emphasis on the fair sharing of risk. Member states adopted different risk thresholds that became evident in the caveats and restrictions some nations placed on the deployment and use of forces. These ensured that, although U.S. allies in the Alliance, notably Canada, the United Kingdom (UK), Holland, France, Italy, Poland, and Germany, were all making significant contributions, the operation did "nothing to suggest that a more equitable burden-sharing relationship between the U.S. and its European allies had emerged."[32] As ISAF expanded its mission in 2005-06, the strategic incoherence and disparities in capabilities that were already evident became further magnified. As Bird and Marshall noted:

> A combination of the alliance principles that 'costs lie where they fall' . . . and the embryonic recognition of a growing insurgency threat ensured that the perennial problem of turning promises into forces on the ground asserted itself.[33]

Yet, while much of the criticism focused on European contributions to ground operations in Afghanistan, there was also a feeling in some quarters that U.S. leadership of NATO had been found wanting, not least because the war in Iraq had occupied much of the administration's political energy.[34]

As President Bush prepared to leave office, scholars and commentators debated whether the transatlantic bargain would endure beyond his administration. G. John Ikenberry suggested that the "crisis" in

transatlantic relations would result either in the breakdown of the Atlantic order, the transformation of that
order leading to major restructuring and a new set of
arrangements, or adaptation of the order, involving
neither complete breakdown nor major restructuring,
but rather a reworking of the bargain to accommodate
new realities, with basic arrangements left intact.[35]
Thomas Risse also suggested the imperatives of adaptation for the Alliance, which would seek to enhance
NATO's relationship with the EU, as well as foster a
revised "transatlantic bargain" involving fundamental change to norms and institutions.[36] Although the
"shock" of 9/11 neither ruptured the bargain nor ren-
dered it irrelevant, it did serve to expose and magnify
existing fault lines and cleavages within the Alliance,
placing them under immense strain. New fault lines
and fissures arose in the context of operations in Afghanistan and Iraq, all of which generated a heightened sense of "crisis" within the Alliance, and a growing consensus in Washington that imbalances within
the Alliance and its increasing fragmentation were
becoming unsustainable. By 2009, NATO was being
conceptualized as a "multi-tier" alliance "in which coalitions of like-minded allies find it increasingly hard
to agree on, let alone execute, strategy."[37]

In response to the deterioration in transatlantic relations, Bush's second term saw a change in approach,
as key officials such as Condoleezza Rice, Kurt Volker,
and Daniel Friedman made a concerted effort to reach
out to European allies and engage in cooperation on
a range of issues. The replacement of Donald Rums-
feld with Robert Gates as Secretary of Defense in 2006
also signaled a shift in approach, with the polarizing
rhetoric of the first term largely dissipating, replaced
with far greater efforts at consensus-building. Still,

by the time Obama took office, America's relationship with NATO appeared mired in a repetitive and frustrating cycle, playing out recurring themes and arguments like a broken record, but with little sense of clarity or resolution to the underlying issues and concerns. In short, the transatlantic bargain that had underpinned the Alliance since 1949 appeared irrevocably weakened by the events and challenges of the post-Cold War era.

## PART II: PARTNERSHIP AND PRAGMATISM: OBAMA AND THE TRANSATLANTIC ALLIANCE

Obama's candidacy appeared, in the first instance, to offer a glimmer of hope that a new spirit of cooperation and harmony could be restored to transatlantic relations. Obama sought a clear and decisive break from the policies and approach of the Bush administration, believing that under Bush's leadership, America's international reputation, credibility, and legitimacy had diminished. Obama had positioned himself during his early political career as an opponent of the Iraq War, and he rejected what he saw as the administration's intolerance of international institutions. In numerous speeches and policy statements, Obama repeated the core themes of his world view, at the heart of which was the notion of renewed American leadership and a new era of global cooperation. During the campaign, Obama pledged to "restore our moral standing so that America is once again that last best hope for all who are called to the cause of freedom. . . ."[38] In an article for *Foreign Affairs* in July 2007, Obama stated his goal "to renew American leadership in the world" through rebuilding international alliances and institutions.[39]

However, it was Obama's Berlin speech that truly galvanized European and international public opinion—by outlining his vision of a "world that stands as one." Acknowledging the differences that had led Europe and America to drift apart, he argued that the "the burdens of global citizenship continue to bind us together," requiring allies who would "listen to each other, learn from each other and, most of all, trust each other."[40] It was Obama's Berlin speech that also articulated most forcefully the cosmopolitanism that appeared to be at the heart of Obama's world view, centered on his "dual identity as an American citizen and a citizen of the world."[41] Cosmopolitan thinking garnered renewed emphasis after 9/11 as part of a wider, reflective debate within U.S. society as to the causation and meaning of the attacks—particularly in light of the strong sense of nationalism and patriotism they generated. Some put forward ideas for "cosmopolitan citizens" and calls for a shift away from an aggressive nationalism to a softer humanism that could inform America's response.[42]

Obama saw himself occupying a "post-ideological" world, one which required new global initiatives and arrangements, including a revitalized NATO.[43] He described the essence of foreign policy as "forging a new relationship with the world based on mutual respect and mutual interest."[44] His was a cosmopolitan world-view based on an:

> intuitive understanding that the United States was unable to impose its own moral and historical narrative on the rest of the world. Obama asserted the American narrative and was unabashedly proud of it; he was an authentic American nationalist. But he did not imagine that he could make progress with the rest of the world dependent on the world sharing that narrative.[45]

Yet, nor did Obama reject the dominant leitmotifs of U.S. foreign policy; he continued to assert the importance of U.S. global leadership and made clear his willingness to use military force when necessary. What he did reject was the ideologically charged zeal for democracy promotion of his predecessor. In this regard, he positioned himself as a "rare bird—a democratic foreign policy realist,"[46] someone who understood the limitations on U.S. power in the world, and preferred a foreign policy based on hard-headed calculations of what was in America's national interest. In many ways, Obama defied easy categorization, appearing to combine youthful idealism and a cosmopolitan world view with a sober realism and scholarly intellect. The latter ensured a tendency to assess each problem on its merits, giving rise to perceptions of the new President as a pragmatist. According to Charles Kupchan, Obama's pragmatism was guided by a set of questions: "What's the problem? How do we fix it? Who will help the United States fix it?"[47] It was through this lens that Obama viewed NATO. As someone unencumbered by the baggage of NATO's history, Obama saw the organization in functionalist terms, as an instrument that could serve America's interests in an interconnected world, and as a vehicle for enhanced burden sharing and partnership.

**Obama's War.**

One of the principal challenges Obama inherited in taking office was the war in Afghanistan. As noted earlier, Obama took office at a time when discourse over the Alliance was dominated by notions of "crisis," with both Nicholas Burns and Robert Gates having made scathing criticisms of the Alliance in February 2008. Still, Obama had made clear during the campaign he believed the Bush administration had "taken its eye off the ball" in switching the focus of U.S. efforts from Afghanistan to Iraq. Once elected, the President thus set about attempting to distance himself from his predecessor, rejecting the Bush administration's sweeping rhetoric of democratization and favoring instead a refocusing of the mission on narrower objectives. In March 2009, Obama stated, "I want the American people to understand that we have a clear and focused goal: to disrupt, dismantle and defeat Al Qaeda in Pakistan and Afghanistan." Obama ordered 21,000 troops to Afghanistan, the largest increase since the war began in 2001. But this was also coupled with a call for a "dramatic increase in our civilian effort" and a pledge that he would "seek civilian support from our partners and allies."[48]

The refocusing of the war in Afghanistan did not represent a radical departure from Bush's policy, but rather a more subtle change in strategy, and it was one with which Obama was entirely comfortable.[49] Obama also made a concerted effort to reach out to America's NATO allies and repair what the administration felt was a significant degree of damage wrought by his predecessor to the transatlantic alliance; Obama's National Security Advisor General James Jones suggested that the administration aimed to "rebalance the relationship, make people feel like they are contributing even a small amount, but to make them feel like they're valued and respected."[50]

This shift in strategy and approach was an important one for NATO. Although Obama hoped that European allies would respond to the troop commitments with their own increase, he also grasped that continuing to lecture European allies on the issue was not a viable long-term option. As a result, the Obama administration placed far more emphasis in early-2009 on asking European nations to focus on what they could do—increasing funding and resources for civilian reconstruction. Jeremy Shapiro, a State Department adviser on Europe, commented that "the tone of the messages he is giving is a specific and intended sharp break with the past."[51]

In February 2009, Vice-President Joseph Biden gave a speech to the 45th Munich Conference on Security Policy in which he made clear the "new tone" that the Obama administration intended to set in its relations with Europe. However, Biden also clarified that in return for the new tone and approach of the Obama administration, the United States would expect more from its partners.[52] In one sense, here was at least a partial attempt on the part of the new administration to recalibrate the bargain; Obama recognized that U.S. leadership of the Alliance required a more nuanced approach than to simply berate European allies over burden sharing, and that, in the context of modern military operations, Europeans had valuable contributions to make. At the same time, he was reminding Europeans that the bargain had always implied a *quid pro quo* and that in return for a more nuanced U.S. leadership, he expected Europeans to respond in kind.

Only 2 weeks later, U.S. aspirations of a more equal partnership were shattered when Gates was told at a meeting of NATO defense ministers in Krakow, Poland, that additional Europeans troops for ISAF would not be forthcoming. This announcement led one commentator to suggest that the administration's message had been "lost in translation."[53] Despite this setback, the Obama administration continued to promote its new strategy for Afghanistan to

NATO, centered on a more comprehensive approach that fused troop increases with more funding and resources for promoting better governance, police training, the rule of law, and economic development. This shift in thinking had begun during the Bush administration, with the publication in 2006 of the U.S. military's new manual *Field Manual (FM) 3-24, Counterinsurgency* (COIN), co-authored by General David Petraeus. Still, it was the Obama administration that found itself largely responsible for developing and implementing the new approach. Its commitment to what it termed "smart power," combining military power with the softer tools of diplomacy, negotiation, and statecraft to achieve U.S. goals and objectives, also meshed well with an emerging consensus in Washington. Such a consensus held that achieving security and stability in the region depended upon a more holistic approach, coupled with increasing engagement with Afghanistan's neighbors, including Iran and Pakistan. It was also music to the ears of many Europeans who had been frustrated by what they perceived as an excessive focus on military power by the Bush administration.

As a result, by the time Alliance leaders gathered in Strasbourg, Germany, for NATO's 60th anniversary summit, Obama had managed to extract promises of troops, military trainers, and civilian experts from America's European allies in what *The Washington Post* called a "sweeping demonstration of support for the new administration's leadership."[54] French President Nicholas Sarkozy welcomed the new approach, commenting:

> It feels really good to work with a U.S. president . . . who understands that the world doesn't boil down to simply American frontiers and borders.[55]

NATO pledged to establish a NATO Training Mission in Afghanistan (NTM-A) to help train the Afghan National Army and Police. But tensions and disagreements refused to disappear as it became evident the troop increases Obama had hoped for would not be forthcoming, puncturing the otherwise celebratory atmosphere at Strasbourg.[56] Sarkozy dismissed a reporter's comment that the United States was sending in more troops while the Europeans were not, by suggesting that "It is the European vision that is triumphing," a reference to the long-standing European desire to focus on civilian reconstruction, rather than military force.[57]

Obama's decision in December 2009 to commit a further 30,000 troops to Afghanistan further fueled tensions in the Alliance. The decision was the result of "the most detailed presidential review of a national security decision since the 1962 Cuban Missile Crisis."[58] Although General Petraeus sought an additional 10,000 U.S. troops, Obama warned him to "Be careful how you characterize our NATO allies. We need them. They will be useful in this coalition."[59] Nevertheless, the 3 months that Obama took to reach his decision became a source of concern, especially in London, UK, and Paris, France, where reports suggested both the British and French governments were growing impatient with what U.S. Republicans had already labeled Obama's "dithering." Bernard Kouchner, the French foreign minister, suggested a lack of leadership from Washington was hampering the Afghan mission and asked, "What is the goal? What is the road? And in the name of what? Where are the Americans? It begins to be a problem."[60]

According to Heather Conley of the Center for Strategic and International Studies, the reaction in Europe to the eventual decision to implement a "surge" was "Wait. You're going to do this again? You're going to ask for more?"[61] This was exactly what the Obama administration did as it made clear that it expected NATO allies to play their part. At a meeting of NATO defense ministers, the Alliance pledged in the region of 7,000 troops, but the response from individual nations was muted; only Britain and Poland offered to increase their troop numbers immediately, while others, including France, Germany, and Italy, were noncommittal. The Germans responded to Obama's deliberations by stating "We will take our own time to assess what he said and discuss this with our allies."[62]

Although Secretary of State Hillary Clinton claimed she was "extremely heartened"[63] by the demonstration of Alliance solidarity, the problem for the administration was that the shift in strategy, although welcomed by many in Europe, could not overcome deeply embedded opposition to the war among European populations. A PEW survey of May-June 2009 found that in Germany, a country with the third largest contingent of Allied troops in Afghanistan, nearly 6-in-10 people favored withdrawal. In most of the other countries surveyed, including France, Britain, Poland, and Spain, the survey found majorities or pluralities opposed to NATO's Afghan mission. While 57 percent of Americans surveyed wanted U.S. troops to stay in Afghanistan, opinion was more evenly divided in Britain, France, and Germany.[64]

In the face of domestic political realities confronting many European allies, Obama's change in tone and approach had only a limited impact. Following the London Afghanistan conference in January 2010,

NATO did confirm that it would commit a total of 7,000 extra troops for ISAF;[65] still, the European failure to respond more positively to Obama's overtures left some observers questioning not only the utility of the Alliance for the United States, but also Obama's leadership. Kori Schake, a former Bush official and Hoover Institution fellow, claimed the "coolness" in the European response "has come as a surprise. And it does matter." For Schake, the explanation for this response lay not in Obama's perceived lack of Atlanticism, but in the overinflated expectations he had of what Europe would be able to deliver. She observed that "President Obama's expectations for the kind of partners Europeans were going to be were far grander than Europe was prepared to deliver."[66]

The resistance the Obama administration encountered led Gates to launch a withering attack on America's European allies at a February 2010 meeting of NATO officials, lamenting what he saw as the "demilitarization of Europe."[67] Even Clinton joined the fray in calling for an "honest discussion" and warned NATO that it risked becoming a "talking shop."[68] Gates's remarks, although scathing in their criticism, were not new, but reflected deep-seated U.S. frustrations with NATO that had been evident since the dawning of the Cold War. Gates would repeat these frustrations in his final speech to NATO in June 2011, where he reminded NATO defense ministers that he was only one in a long line of U.S. Defense Secretaries "exasperated" at the failure of some members of the Alliance to meet agreed-upon NATO benchmarks for spending. He also warned the Alliance that if it did not establish a more equitable burden-sharing arrangement, it faced "the very real possibility of collective military irrelevance."[69]

Gates's comments were clearly intended to inject a sense of urgency into debates over Alliance burden sharing for a European audience; they did not, however, paint an entirely fair or accurate picture. As noted earlier, the comprehensive nature of modern military operations has required a greater emphasis on contributions to the civilian dimension of the operations, such as policing and economic reconstruction. When it comes to ISAF, NATO's European allies accounted for almost 60 percent of the armed forces committed, with Canada contributing 33 percent, and the United States less than 2 percent. In addition, European NATO Allies have made major contributions when it comes to aid and development assistance.[70] Although such contributions are recognized and acknowledged in Washington, the tendency to focus on more traditional measures of burden sharing, notably defense spending, can obscure the very real and important contributions European allies make.

In this regard, NATO Secretary General Anders Fogh Rasmussen was right when he noted that U.S. claims that "Europeans do too little" simply do not paint the full picture.[71] Moreover, one might argue that the more normative and holistic approach to security of many in Europe provides a critical counterpoint to the militarism that has tended to typify U.S. attitudes to defense.[72] Making sweeping generalizations about the "pacification" of Europe is also inherently problematic—not least because "Europe" is not a homogeneous entity, but a coming together of a myriad of different strategic cultures, all with differing views on the use of military force. Some European nations, notably Britain, have greater synergy with an American way of thinking, while the Obama administration put a renewed emphasis on soft (or "smart") power and civilian tools and capabilities, as reflected in the release of the first *Quadrennial Diplomacy and Development Review* (QDDR) in 2010.[73]

## A New Urgency.

Despite the nuances and complexities injected into the transatlantic bargain in a post-Cold War world, the bargain continues to be undermined, as far as Washington is concerned, by a number of interrelated gaps that have emerged within the Alliance over the past 2 decades. With U.S. defense spending increasing in the context of the war on terror and sharp cuts to many European defense budgets prompted by the 2008 economic crisis, a defense spending gap had emerged by 2010 that was, in turn, fueling a growing capabilities gap within the Alliance. As defense expert Hans Binnendijk noted in testimony to Congress ahead of NATO's 2012 Chicago summit, in 2011 "NATO's European members averaged just 1.6 percent of GDP or $282.9 billion spent on defense while the United States spent 4.8 percent of GDP or $685.6 billion on defense," equating to "69 percent and 28 percent of total NATO defense spending for European NATO members and the United States, respectively."[74] Across the board, the defense expenditure of the European NATO Allies is forecast to decline by 2.9 percent (after adjusting for inflation) between 2010 and 2015.[75]

By contrast, between 2001-12 U.S. defense spending was on an upward trajectory, thus ensuring both a widening defense spending gap between the United States and Europe, as well as a growing capabilities gap; while the United States had continued to invest in high-end technology and expeditionary capabilities, many European nations had made only modest improvements.[76] Added to this is a transformation gap; while the U.S. military undertook a major process of transformation after the end of the Cold War, European militaries have lagged behind. Despite the transformation agenda instituted at the 2002 Prague Summit, there have been significant disparities across Europe in the pace and scope of transformation, due to the different time scales Allies have adopted, national domestic politics, and the different ways in which the Allies have interpreted the transformation agenda.[77]

However, U.S. frustration with the Alliance became more sustained after 9/11, imbalances in capabilities and burden sharing, although unpalatable and frequently lamented, were begrudgingly tolerated because: a) America's dominant position within the Alliance continued to serve U.S. interests; and, b) there was no urgent economic imperative to scale back Alliance spending or contributions. This was the essence of the transatlantic bargain that underpinned the Alliance through the Cold War and into the post-Cold War years. As noted earlier, the bargain underwent minor adjustments in the 1990s; U.S. troop levels in Europe saw some reductions, and Europe accelerated efforts to forge closer integration in the security and defense realm. Calls for a more substantive revision of the transatlantic bargain in the absence of the Soviet threat were offset, however, by instability in Europe and a U.S. foreign policy agenda that gave primacy to the core task of preserving and advancing stability, security, and democracy across an expanding Europe. In the light of limited progress in European defense integration and transformation, which left NATO as the principal mechanism for guaranteeing European security, as well as of a decade of relative prosperity, Washington's interests continued to be served by maintaining its role as *primus inter pares* within the Alliance.

Obama, however, was elected at a time when a confluence of factors served to cast doubt on the ongoing value, and sustainability, of America retaining its hegemonic role within the Alliance. In broader terms, the nature of U.S. global leadership and the centrality of Europe as a whole to U.S. strategic thinking were being called into question. Obama entered office acutely aware of the limitations of American power—and of its willingness and ability to continue to act as a "global policeman" in the face of enormous economic challenges at home. Obama intuitively grasped the significance for the United States of China's increasingly prominent role on the world stage. With concern growing among America's allies in the Asia-Pacific over China's rising power, and with concern growing within Washington over challenges to U.S. primacy in the region, the Obama administration was naturally less focused on Europe as a region.[78]

This strategic rebalancing was part of an evolutionary process that had been under way since the end of the Cold War. Both the Clinton and George W. Bush administrations had accorded a high priority to the Asia-Pacific; indeed, a perennial debate in foreign policy circles through the 1990s and 2000s was the relative merits of "containment" versus "engagement" with a rising China. The strategic significance of the Greater Middle East was also heightened in the post-Cold War years, in the context of ongoing instability and turmoil and the ever-increasing domestic demand for the free flow of energy supplies from the region. As regional stability in the Asia-Pacific and Middle East took on greater significance for the United States, Europe conversely undertook a gradual process of expansion and, over the last decade in particular, a more sustained effort to forge a European security and defense capability. The events of 9/11 only served to further shift America's strategic focus away from Europe and toward what Zbigniew Brzezinski had more than 2 decades earlier termed an "arc of crisis."[79]

Unlike Presidents Clinton and Bush, however, Obama had to contend with an economic crisis the likes of which America had not experienced since the Great Depression; originating in the U.S. subprime mortgage market, this crisis served to expose the fragility of the American economy and was a painful reminder of America's vulnerability—and of the urgent need to set America's "house in order." As a result, the need to both reduce U.S. defense spending and continue America's strategic reprioritization was paramount during Obama's first 2 years in office. This was simply a pragmatic response for the United States to a world in which "Europe is no longer an object of security concern as it was during the Cold War and its immediate aftermath."[80] With the United States seeking to scale back its global commitments and further rebalance toward the Asia-Pacific, it naturally looked to Europe to take on greater responsibility for security in its own backyard—and especially for crises or conflicts in which the United States had only minimal strategic interests at stake.

It was against this backdrop that the Alliance found itself having to confront the prospect of yet another military operation, this time in Libya. Unlike in Afghanistan, however, the conflict was on the European periphery, and vital U.S. national interests were not at stake. During the 1990s, conflicts in the Balkans had proven beyond the capacity of Europe to deal with alone, with the United States playing a major role in terms of both military contributions and political leadership. By 2011 and the eruption of another violent conflict on Europe's periphery, the context was very different: the United States was war-weary, suffering from military overstretch, and facing a challenging domestic economic context—all of which mitigated against the United States playing a leading role and brought into even sharper focus the need for a rethinking of the transatlantic bargain.

### Leadership from Behind?

With the Obama administration acutely aware of the toll two major military engagements in Afghanistan and Iraq had taken, as well as of the damage to its international reputation and standing in the Arab world, and with the administration forced to confront the most challenging economic crisis since the Great Depression, the political and public appetite for U.S. involvement in Libya was limited, at best. The crisis in Libya, taking place in the heart of the European "neighborhood," represented an opportunity for European members of the Alliance to "step up" and demonstrate their ability and willingness to assume a greater leadership role. Despite his initial reluctance to intervene, as the situation on the ground deteriorated and with Britain and France pushing forcefully for a no-fly zone, Obama began to call for a broader resolution that would authorize military force against Muammar Qadaffi's forces. The result was Operation ODYSSEY DAWN, a series of air strikes commencing on March 19, 2011, carried out by the United States, the UK, and France but under U.S. strategic command. The United States then handed over command and control to NATO for Operation UNIFIED PROTECTOR on March 31.

The operation was, in many ways, a perfect demonstration of the Obama administration's broader approach to foreign policy, one centered on the concepts of partnership and pragmatism.[81] Despite the lack of an overwhelming strategic rationale for U.S. military engagement, it was hard for the Obama administration to turn a blind eye to the moral imperatives for action, particularly in the context of earlier efforts to reach out to and engage the Arab world. But with domestic support limited and defense cuts looming on the horizon, the administration also could not play the kind of dominant role it had done in previous Alliance operations. Thus, Obama was keen to make clear that, while the United States would "focus our unique capabilities on the front end of the operation," it would then move to a "supporting role." It would seek to "transfer responsibility to our allies and partners" to ensure that "the risk and cost of this operation — to our military and to American taxpayers — will be reduced significantly." Obama also maintained that "real leadership created the conditions and coalitions for others to step up as well — to work with allies and partners so that they could bear their share of the burden and pay their share of the costs."[82] In this regard, "the U.S. approach to the campaign . . . reflected America's logic of a new transatlantic burden-sharing model in the light of a changed grand strategy."[83] Still, despite the pragmatism that drove such logic, the Obama administration was accused of "eschewing its indispensible role of leadership"[84] within the Alliance, in what was unflatteringly depicted as "leadership from behind."[85]

This criticism came about partly because the United States withheld some critical capabilities, such as the A-10 *Thunderbolt II* and AC-130 *Specter* gunships, but also because, while such logic made perfect sense in theory, it proved harder to implement in practice. Although Britain, France, and a handful of other European allies provided the bulk of combat sorties, the United States was forced to step in and supply key enabling assets, including the U.S. joint surveillance target attack radar system (JSTARS) and airborne warning and control system (AWACS) aircraft.

Yet, even this fact could not hide what appeared to be a stepchange in U.S. attitudes to the Alliance. As a major *RUSI* study of the operation argued:

> Despite its established history of leading 'coalitions of the willing,' with commitments elsewhere and resource challenges of its own, the Libya campaign was a clear example of the U.S. seeking to play a different role.[86]

America's NATO allies also demonstrated that there were indeed possibilities for a new transatlantic bargain, one in which European members of the Alliance — as well as NATO partners — would take on increasing roles and responsibilities.

As Binnendijk pointed out to Congress in testimony prior to the 2012 Chicago Summit, 90 percent of all ordinance dropped on Libya was delivered by Europeans.[87] Moreover, not only did France and Britain demonstrate their willingness to "step up," but so, too, did a number of smaller European nations that contributed vital niche capabilities, including Norway, Belgium, Italy, and Denmark. Qatar, the United Arab Emirates, Morocco, Jordan, and Sweden also played key operational roles. As one U.S. commentator conceded:

> Libya shows Americans that Europe and Canada are not denuded, post-modern pacifists. In this battle,

Europeans took the lead, demonstrating that they can and will use force when they have the political will to do so.[88]

Although it is unwise to portray the Libyan operation as a harbinger of future trends, it is also hard not to conclude that it does mark a shift in the dynamics of U.S. leadership of the Alliance—not least because, as one U.S. official conceded, "Our ability to carry the burden is being called into question."[89]

Still, the reliance of many European nations on the United States for critical assets gave rise to the view that:

> The Europeans were counting too heavily on the United States for their security at a time when Americans were increasingly preoccupied with advancing their strategic interests in Asia and the Pacific. In short, the perception grew that the trans-Atlantic link was weakening.[90]

Secretary Gates further fueled such perceptions when he warned, in the midst of Operation UNIFIED PROTECTOR, that in the context of ongoing imbalances in burden sharing and capabilities the Alliance faced the prospect of increasing irrelevance.[91] Such warnings were followed by more tangible signs that the mood in Washington was firmly shifting. In January 2012, the United States released its *Defense Strategic Guidance* (DSG), which confirmed an expected reduction in U.S. forces in Europe and a strategic focus on the Asia-Pacific, as well as announcing substantial defense cuts of a projected $487 billion over the next decade.[92] As a result, U.S. defense spending is set to decline for the first time in 13 years. Although this will reduce the defense spending gap with many Allies, it is also a clear signal that the United States will be less willing and able to contribute to European security to the same degree as in the past.

The DSG was released against a backdrop of growing congressional disquiet over Alliance disparities. Congressional skepticism of the Alliance has always been a key dynamic influencing U.S.-NATO relations. This is particularly true today, at a time when congressional scrutiny and criticism of America's commitment to NATO has intensified, and is taking on a new salience in the context of the campaign in Libya, the global financial crisis, and U.S. defense cuts. According to one U.S. congressman:

> We're fighting at this level and they're at another level and that comes down to investment, hardware, training, personnel and making it a priority. And to some extent my constituents, those who pay attention to such issues, I think they're troubled by the free-rider aspect of this.[93]

As previously noted, such claims do not paint a wholly accurate picture. Although there had been a widening spending gap between the United States and many of its Allies prior to 2012, some analysts did indeed question "whether it is not really a matter of the United States spending too much on defense, rather than the Europeans spending too little." Furthermore, while the capabilities gap may also have widened, this "pales in significance when one considers they are allied with each other, are qualitatively compatible, and have capabilities that complement the other's shortfalls."[94] Still, this has not prevented Congress from demanding more equitable burden sharing. In 2012, Congress called on Europe not only to shoulder a larger share of NATO's missile defense program, but also:

to reduce the defense gap with the United States by equipping themselves with capabilities that are deemed to be critical, deployable, and sustainable; to meet the agreed upon benchmark of spending at least 2 percent of Gross Domestic Product (GDP) on defense; and to demonstrate political determination to achieve these goals.[95]

Although the United States pays a share of NATO's commonly funded budget proportionate to its Gross National Income (GNI), only three NATO allies meet the 2 percent agreed-upon benchmark of defense spending as a percentage of GDP.[96] Yet, as noted earlier, this is not a particularly fair or accurate way of measuring burden sharing within the Alliance, a point captured by former Secretary General Jaap de Hoop Scheffer in 2008:

> How does one decide what is a fair contribution from a country of 50 million against a contribution from a country with a population of only 4 million? How can you evaluate a contribution of light infantry against the provision of critical enablers such as helicopters or air-to-air refuellers? And over what time period?[97]

Even so, the transformation gap evident between the United States and many European allies is of increasing concern to Washington. In Norfolk, Virginia, in 2003, as part of NATO's post-9/11 transformation agenda, the Allied Command Transformation (ACT) was posited "to be the forcing agent for change within the Alliance and to act as the focus and motivating force to bring intellectual rigor to the change process."[98] Part of the purpose of ACT was to accelerate the transformation of member-state forces from being rooted in a conventional Cold War mindset, into lighter, faster, and more rapidly deployable forces capable of conducting expeditionary operations alongside U.S. forces. ACT was originally co-located with the U.S. Joint Forces Command (USJFCOM), and, as Cornish notes, "many of the intellectual, technological and doctrinal roots for the military transformation agenda are derived specifically from the US experience."[99]

In practice, however, Alliance transformation has not proceeded at the pace nor the scope that the United States had hoped. By the mid-to-late-2000s, key officials were expressing concern that ACT's transformation process lacked a wider strategic framework to give it coherence and "an understanding of the problem that needed to be solved."[100] In addition, the pace of transformation varied across European capitals; some countries, like Britain and France, had already begun transforming their militaries in the early-1990s, but many had not. In practice, it proved harder to transfer U.S. concepts and practices into an alliance framework. In September 2009, France took over command of ACT, while in 2011, the United States disestablished the USJFCOM. Although efforts have been made to tailor ACT's transformation more specifically to the requirements of member states, the result has been a failure to close the transformation gap in the way the United States had hoped and envisaged in 2003.[101]

Although the United States recognized that Alliance transformation is an ongoing process rather than an end in itself, its decision to reduce its own defense spending has further added to the uncertainty over how such gaps can be closed. In January 2012, Obama's Ambassador to NATO Ivo Daalder warned that, "If there ever was a time in which the

United States could always be counted on to fill the gaps that may emerge in European defense, that time is rapidly coming to an end."[102] Yet, neither should such criticism be seen as evidence that the United States is in danger of turning its back on the Alliance nor that there is a growing and irreparable rupture in U.S.-NATO relations. Thomas Ries wrongly paints a picture of NATO as a sinking ship whose "captain" has already jumped overboard.[103] Such views fail to acknowledge that persistent U.S. criticism of the Alliance is not only nothing new, but is also possible only because of the underlying strength of the transatlantic bargain, which allows for an honest and frank exchange of views. When Gates gave his farewell speech to the Alliance in June 2011—a speech that contained some forthright and robust criticisms of NATO—he took pains to point out that:

> I share these views in the spirit of solidarity and friendship, with the understanding that true friends occasionally must speak bluntly with one another for the sake of those greater interests and values that bind us together.[104]

**A Transatlantic Bargain for the 21st Century.**

On both sides of the Atlantic, however, there is a growing consensus concerning the need for a revised transatlantic agreement.[105] In his seminal piece on the transatlantic bargain, Cleveland wrote that "While the bargain changes, the constant is a consensus among the allies that there has to be a bargain." This remains as true today as it did then. But as Cleveland also acknowledged:

> Unless the Europeans have a lively interest in their own defense, it becomes politically impossible

for a government in Washington to represent to its own people that we are partners in a collective security mission.[106]

As noted earlier, European integration has accelerated since the end of the Cold War, and a "lively interest" in European defense has clearly been in evidence. But Washington has not always made it easy for its European allies, at times remaining suspicious of European integration in security and defense matters. Although those suspicions are waning, Washington continues to view NATO as the principal mechanism for transatlantic security affairs.

Moreover, while Washington wants—and indeed expects—greater burden sharing within the Alliance, with European members playing a greater role both in terms of political will and military capabilities, it is not willing to relinquish its dominant leadership role entirely. U.S. officials continue to view America's role within the Alliance as that of the "indispensible nation."[107] Such a label is not entirely misplaced; U.S. leadership of the Alliance remains vital for its overall health and endurance, and, if Libya proved anything, it was the reality that at present, European air forces are incapable of conducting a major strategic air campaign without U.S. help. Moreover, for larger-scale conflicts farther afield, the Alliance will invariably "need to rely on more significant American support than was the case in Libya."[108] However, the United States will also not continue to tolerate the culture of dependency that has afflicted the Alliance throughout its history. The withdrawal of two U.S. Army combat brigades from Europe may raise concerns over the ability of U.S. and European forces to sustain levels of interoperability,[109] but it should be regarded as an opportunity for the dynamics of leadership within the Alliance to shift toward a more "post-American" alliance. It is important to note that this shift does not mean an absence of U.S. leadership, or even a diminution of it, but rather, as Damon Wilson describes it, "the right mix of U.S. leadership, European ambition, and stronger global partnerships."[110] It requires both the United States and its NATO allies in Europe and Canada to "address transatlantic relations with a clearer eye and a harder head,"[111] wherein the United States encourages and facilitates a substantive process of European members more consciously "stepping up," and NATO partners becoming more visible and influential players.

The term "post-American" may not be a comfortable one for some Americans; it brings with it notions of the limits of U.S. power and leadership, and of a world in which U.S. global hegemony is challenged. It is certainly a far cry from the "American Century" proclaimed by Henry Luce in 1945.[112] However, the 21st century will surely not be dominated by American power in all its forms in quite the same way as the second half of the 20th century was. America, then, has to adapt to new realities; so, too, does the Atlantic Alliance that has bound it to Europe for over half a century. Luce's aphorism was the product of a particular time and place, just as notions of a "post-American" world reflect the changing dynamics of global geopolitics. Still, the term should not be interpreted as evidence of American "decline" or waning global leadership; conversely, it captures a world in which the United States must learn to live—and to lead—alongside other powers.

As far as NATO is concerned, a "post-American" world means a different kind of burden sharing and enhanced partnering within an Alliance that casts aside Cold War patterns of dependency. For large-scale operations, in which core U.S. national interests are at stake, the United States will no doubt continue to play a dominant role within the Alliance. America's unwavering commitment to transformation, fostering interoperability, and enhancing engagement and out-reach with NATO partners will ensure that it contin-ues to act as an engine driving the Alliance forward. But for those operations in which core U.S. interests are not at stake, "Europe should expect a relative-ly reduced U.S. role, and a greater role for its own forces."[113] As the United States makes hard strategic choices over where its priorities and strategic focus lie, it will need to balance ongoing leadership in, and commitment to, Europe and NATO with the demands and requirements of its focus on the Asia-Pacific and its enduring interests in the Greater Middle East. U.S. foreign policy is not a zero-sum game: a "pivot" to Asia-Pacific does not mean a turning away from Eu-rope, nor does the current focus on a rising China mean that Europe is somehow marginalized. More-over, as Zbigniew Brzezinski has claimed, European power politics could come back to haunt the United States, and NATO provides a crucial entry point for the United States into Eurasia.[114]

However, a revised transatlantic bargain does re-quire a willingness on the part of European allies to take on greater leadership roles and responsibilities when the opportunity arises. This may well, as in the case of Libya, involve support from Washington; it is likely that a new bargain will be characterized by a "flexible geometry" approach to missions, whereby groups of nations come together to act, depending on the nature and type of mission. Such an approach may well permit some nations to opt out—as did Germany and Poland in the case of Libya—but it is an approach that better reflects NATO's evolution into "a complex security network rather than a traditional alliance."[115] While Europe's larger powers, such as France and Britain, might take on more active and visible leadership roles, smaller European nations will also likely contribute niche capabilities, while NATO partners will also play important roles. That the Alliance is today viewed as a hub of a network of security partnerships is in no small part due to a U.S. desire and determination to see NATO take on such a role. The Obama administration's focus on encouraging greater burden sharing and an expanded network of partnerships for the Alliance is entirely commensurate with its broader strategic approach. In recent years, the United States has increasingly come to value NATO as a tool for partnership and the sharing and exchange of information and expertise, including on issues such as counter-improvised explosive device (IED) work. As one senior NATO official at ACT commented in 2011:

> Capability development transformation is happening in partnership with the U.S. in a much better way . . . the more that the U.S. sees that there are opportunities to partner with NATO . . . they get quite excited.[116]

An enhanced role for NATO partners is central to any revised transatlantic bargain. Such partnerships had developed prior to 9/11, but the war in Afghanistan undoubtedly served to magnify their influence and significance. While the invitation of 13 of these partners to Chicago was a symbolic appreciation of their contributions, it remains to be seen how such partnerships will evolve and develop in the absence of major operational activity. The issue of NATO partnerships is critical to the Alliance's future, not least because they are intertwined with a number of other issues, including burden sharing, the challenges posed by an era of austerity, and U.S. strategic rebalancing. Regarding the latter, the partners in the Asia-Pacific, including Australia, Japan, and South Korea, are likely to take on increased importance; as a result, NATO needs to think more strategically and systematically about how far, and in what ways, it engages with regions beyond the Euro-Atlantic zone. The Alliance has struggled to decide to what degree those partners outside of formal Alliance mechanisms such as the Euro-Atlantic Partnership Council (EAPC), Istanbul Cooperation Initiative (ICI), and Mediterranean Dialogue (MD) should be engaged with. NATO's focus on Afghanistan over the past decade has largely allowed it to defer such issues; as Benjamin Schreer notes:

> The value of these partnerships has largely been these countries' contributions to the Afghanistan mission. However, with the ISAF mission gradually coming to a close, the question is how these relationships can be further developed beyond Afghanistan.[117]

Countries like Australia remain unsure how seriously NATO is regarding engagement in the Asia-Pacific. This is not surprising, given that the Alliance itself has little clear sense of its own identity. As the United States seeks to reposition itself in a multipolar world, so, too, must the Alliance. As far as Washington is concerned, NATO should continue to mold itself as a more explicitly "global" Alliance, fostering greater outreach and engagement with like-minded partners, and safeguarding transatlantic interests beyond the Euro-Atlantic zone. In the context of recent events across the Arab world and the ongoing challenge posed by Iran, it makes sense for the Alliance to forge closer partnerships with the Gulf Cooperation Council (GCC) and the countries of the Middle East and North Africa region (MENA).[118] It was notable that the Alliance's new partnership policy, unveiled in Chicago, did not include plans for a global partnership forum and made reference to "partners across the globe," rather than "global partners." Such a distinction may be mere semantics, but it does reflect the unease among some members about the idea of a "global" NATO. However, in its reference to the potential for wider engagement with "any nation across the globe that shares our interest in peaceful international relations," the policy opens up the possibility of establishing closer ties with countries such as India and China. Whether or not this happens, it is clear that NATO is entering a significant phase in its partnership development. As partners become further integrated into structured partnership programs and cooperation increases, they will become important players in a revised transatlantic bargain.

For the Obama administration, the Alliance's future relevance lies in its ability to recognize that the world around it has changed—and to adapt accordingly. A move toward a more post-American Alliance would be a step in the right direction. It offers the prospect of an Alliance that recognizes America's need to shift its focus away from Europe, without fearing a waning of U.S. commitment. It provides an opportunity for America's allies and partners within the Alliance to play ever-more-prominent and visible roles, through the development of niche capabilities and Alliance-wide capabilities, with the United States acting in a supporting and enabling capacity when appropriate. The move recognizes that old Cold War patterns of dependency cannot be sustained and that there is a need for NATO to "mature," but still continue to benefit from U.S. leadership and vision.

### Rethinking the Transatlantic Bargain.

Moving beyond a culture of dependency on U.S. leadership and capabilities in a climate of austerity, in which there is little likelihood of increases in European defense spending or investment, will not be easy. Signs are emerging, however, that the outlines of a revised bargain are already discernible — centered on a firm recognition on both sides of the Atlantic of the need not only for a rebalancing within the Alliance, through mechanisms such as multinational defense collaboration and a greater role for European allies and partners, but also in the broader context of U.S.-NATO-EU relations. The question of defense reform across Europe has grown increasingly salient in light of the economic crisis, but with multiple initiatives taking place — some within NATO, some within the EU, and some bilaterally — a discourse that tends to think of revising the transatlantic bargain only in terms of NATO is unhelpful at best.

What is needed is greater U.S. engagement and leadership on the critical question of forging a more coherent and effective U.S.-NATO-EU partnership. Although it is true to say that "the ideological heat" has been taken out of the debate over EU-NATO, Washington continues to send mixed signals when it comes to the question of a fully autonomous European defense capability separate from NATO.[119] Although the Berlin Plus arrangements of 2003 facilitated a more functional relationship between the EU and NATO, allowing the EU to use NATO's command-and-control assets in operations in which NATO as a whole was not engaged, the arrangement has suffered from a number of limitations. Not the least of these stems from NATO's "right of first refusal," which generated tensions and discord, particularly over EU missions in Africa.[120] The Bush presidency witnessed a shift in U.S. attitudes from the outright skepticism and, at times, hostility that characterized U.S. attitudes during the 1990s. However, the U.S. position has remained somewhat ambivalent, preferring to "guide all decisions on security and defense issues to the North Atlantic Council (NAC), where it rejects any idea of a European caucus, rather than to the Council of the EU." By the end of the Bush administration, the United States thus occupied something of a paradoxical position, favoring NATO over ESDP, but at the same time denigrating the Alliance and frequently lambasting European military inadequacy.[121]

There are signs the Obama administration has strived to adopt a rather more pragmatic and nuanced approach to European security and defense. U.S. Assistant Secretary of State for Europe and Eurasian Affairs Philip H. Gordon has expended considerable time and energy into strengthening bilateral U.S.-EU relations, while France's reintegration into NATO's integrated military command structure in 2009 went a long way toward easing long-standing U.S. concerns over the EU as a possible competitor to NATO. NATO-EU cooperation has been evident in the Balkans, Afghanistan, and Libya, and is generally considered to be very good at the staff-to-staff level.[122] As Secretary Clinton argued, "In the past the U.S. has been ambivalent about whether NATO should engage in security cooperation with the EU. Well, that time is over."[123]

Clinton and Lady Catherine Ashton, the High Representative of the EU for Foreign Affairs and Security Policy, have developed a solid working relationship. The United States and EU are cooperating on a range of issues, including counterpiracy and relations with Turkey, with much greater U.S.-EU engagement at the strategic level. Although Washington continues to prefer military operations to go through NATO, with the EU acting in a "complementary" capacity, and views ACT as the principal mechanism for promoting European defense transformation, the economic crisis and U.S. strategic rebalancing have changed the dynamics of U.S. attitudes to European defense issues. Despite its preference for NATO, Washington is increasingly looking to the EU to "do more" through CSDP, established in Lisbon in 2007.[124] This desire for "Europe to do more" has become an urgent imperative, as the United States faces its own fiscal constraints and looks to shift its force posture. From an American perspective, Europe is at peace and simply no longer requires the kind of U.S. security guarantee that has been the linchpin of the bargain for so long.

That is not to say that the United States does not have vital interests at stake in Europe; indeed, as one of America's closest trading partners, and with its history of shared values, culture, and ideals, Europe continues to be viewed by the United States as its natural partner in the world.[125] Precisely for this reason, it makes sense for Washington to see a more coherent and effective NATO-EU partnership. Although admitting such a partnership remains a "work in progress," the administration has been fully supportive of the efforts of Secretary General Rasmussen and High Representative Ashton.[126] Past concerns that the EU posed a threat to NATO have been replaced by a far more pragmatic and functional approach:

I don't think it's one or the other, it's not zero-sum, it's not as if we do more with NATO that means we need to do less with the EU or vice-versa; it doesn't mean that if we're doing more with the EU in one area, it means that we are taking away from what we're doing with NATO. The U.S. is a member of NATO and in that regard we're always going to look to NATO first on certain issues, but at the same time the EU clearly has a mandate and jurisdiction over certain issues that NATO doesn't.[127]

From a U.S. perspective, it is the U.S.-NATO affiliation that has always been at the center of the transatlantic relationship—a legacy of the Cold War. But as the European integration project has developed over the past 2 decades, such a view of transatlantic relations has become increasingly outdated. That the futures of the EU and NATO are inextricably linked is a recognition not lost on the current administration, which has in recent years come to accept and value the EU as a strategic actor. However, transatlantic relations remain characterized by a tendency to see U.S.-NATO relations and U.S.-EU relations as separate and distinct entities. What is required is a greater understanding of the need to forge a more holistic transatlantic security relationship.

However, concerns rightly remain on both sides of the Atlantic as to the future trajectory of the EU. Not only is there frustration at the inability of the EU to conduct anything more than small-scale, low-end operations and missions; there is also ongoing skepticism over the degree to which the EU will develop into a truly global strategic actor, focused not only internally on its own issues and challenges, but externally—able to stand as a genuine partner alongside the United States in engaging with such global issues as the rise of China.[128] Given the scale of the economic crisis within Europe, active U.S. support for greater European defense integration is necessarily limited, the administration having had to "rationalize what we can expect out of the EU."[129] With the EU mired in the euro-zone crisis, leaders on both sides of the Atlantic have invested much hope and energy in multinational collaboration across Europe; while Europe seeks to engage in pooling and sharing of capabilities through permanent structured cooperation (PESCO), NATO is investing heavily in "smart defense," an issue that was high on the agenda at NATO's Chicago Summit.[130]

Although such collaboration is not new, the increased focus and energy being invested in such projects are evidence that collaboration is seen as an important pillar of a new transatlantic bargain, facilitating a more efficient and coordinated way in which Europe can generate resources and capabilities. A number of concerns remain, however. The 20 or so projects NATO is planning, which include the pooling of maritime patrol aircraft and improving the availability of precision weapons for fighter aircraft, pose some difficult, and as yet unanswered, questions about national sovereignty and the particular mechanisms by which the third strand of smart defense—specialization—can be embedded:

> What is the overall strategic narrative beyond saving money? Should this be a bottom-up process where many small projects eventually create effect, or do NATO Allies need top-down direction and big flagship projects? Finally, can sovereignty concerns and better use of resources be reconciled?[131]

NATO's 2012 Chicago Summit did suggest that progress is at least under way, the Alliance announcing the establishment of its Alliance Ground Surveillance System (AGS), which includes the acquisition of unmanned aerial vehicles. AGS had been an issue of major concern in Washington—given the impasse in reaching an agreement—and one Secretary of Defense Leon Panetta had identified in his first major speech in October 2011 as being a "crucial symbol of alliance collaboration."[132] The Summit declaration on Alliance capabilities also set out plans for *NATO Forces 2020*, a vision for generating "modern, tightly connected forces equipped, trained, exercised and commanded so that they can operate together and with partners in any environment," while the *Connected Forces* initiative spelled out plans to enhance training and education. The declaration also described the Alliance's intention to generate "improvements in the way we develop and deliver the capabilities our missions require."[133]

Still, it was indicative that, in the summit declaration on defense capabilities, only a passing mention was made of the importance of a "changed outlook" and a "renewed culture of cooperation."[134] But how do such a "culture of cooperation" and "changed outlook" become deeply embedded within the Alliance? Former Assistant Secretary General Edgar Buckley has suggested that experiences relating to organizational change in the private and public sector could help foster cultural transformation in NATO. Buckley maintains that the Alliance needs to work at establishing a core set of values "that are explicitly understood and embraced by all members" and "should provide the cultural foundation that will enable NATO to adapt and execute new strategies in an ever changing world." Practical measures that could help embed such change include strengthening the authority of the Secretary General; making better use of social media tools; and fostering enhanced communication, training, and knowledge-sharing mechanisms. Most importantly, the:

> Alliance's leadership must ensure that leaders, commanders, staff, partners, and other stakeholders understand the strategy and goals of NATO's reform effort, and their role in it.[135]

The United States has a clear interest in promoting and advancing multinational defense collaboration across Europe, and ACT has been an important driver of change. Washington must, however, be mindful of not exerting too much pressure on Europeans to 'buy American' and must encourage and promote European defense industry, a process under way via ACT's "Framework for Collaborative Interaction."[136] Perhaps more critically, NATO's reform must also be carried out with the EU in mind; the key challenge remains aligning EU and NATO reform and transformation. The aim of the EU's PESCO is to facilitate groups of states to come together within an EU framework to overcome capability shortfalls, and to give strategic direction and coordination to existing multinational clusters. However, as a report for the CSIS notes, the problem facing both smart defense and PESCO is that "most countries are pursuing sharp reductions on a purely national basis with no reference to NATO or EU obligations or consideration of the overall coherence of the residual posture."[137] In addition, far greater coordination is required between the European Defense Agency (EDA), the coordinating framework for

PESCO, and ACT. But efforts to forge a more effective relationship between EDA and ACT have been persistently hampered by the unresolved Turkey-Cyprus issue, which remains a critical institutional barrier to NATO-EU cooperation on defense investment. As one ACT official conceded, frustrations are rampant on both sides of the Atlantic:

> In our capacity as capability developer we're very well aware that the EU is doing stuff as well, but ACT is not authorised to talk to the EDA unless it has gone through a particular committee which the Turkish are present on. They can therefore judge whether they want to veto the work or not . . . we work around that as best we can . . . but it's totally dysfunctional.[138]

A further issue is the recent bilateral defense agreement between the UK and France. On the one hand, such cooperation is not only logical, but also suggests the possibility of a new Anglo-French defense axis at the heart of Europe that could provide the engine for reinvigorated European leadership in the realm of defense and security. On the other hand, Anglo-French cooperation has to be embedded within the wider European context. For Paddy Ashdown, Anglo-French leadership is crucial. But he conceded it must be part of a wider vision that actively explores cooperation with other European nations, and seeks to foster "an interlocking strategic view as a prelude to common procurement," which can help generate collective capabilities and build a "globally competitive European defence industry."[139]

To be sure, there are signs of better pan-European coordination in defense cooperation and transformation. Despite concern over obstacles to effective cooperation between EDA and ACT, such problems do not mean:

We haven't made a difference because we have been able to expose to the EDA all that NATO is doing in the wake of Lisbon in terms of critical capabilities, IED work, cyber-warfare, missile defence.[140]

In addition, efforts are at last under way to "de-conflict" EU "pooling and sharing" initiatives with NATO's own think tanks. A common agenda and calls to replicate the NATO-EU cells at Supreme Headquarters Allied Powers Europe (SHAPE) and EU Military Staff (EUMS) at EDA and ACT make sense if EDA-ACT cooperation is to be further enhanced.[141] In addition, levels of both formal and informal institutional cooperation between NATO and the EU have developed considerably in recent years. There is now a NATO-EU Capability Group, a NATO Permanent Liaison Team based with the EUMS, and an EU cell based at NATO's SHAPE. The Berlin Plus arrangements, which remain in place for the EU's mission in Bosnia-Herzegovina, Operation ALTHEA, provide for NATO's Deputy SACEUR (DSACEUR) to be operational commander, thus ensuring senior EU defense officials have regular access to the highest echelons of NATO's operational chain of command. Finally, the NATO Secretary General and the EU high representative, along with other senior officials from both institutions, regularly attend each other's meetings, while there are also ad hoc meetings between NATO's NAC and the EU's Political and Security Committee (PSC). NATO representatives from the country hosting the EU's rotating presidency give weekly briefings to the NAC, while a senior EU defense official also regularly briefs senior NATO officials. Informal channels of cooperation have also developed outside of institutional structures, including the vast array of Brussels-based think tanks.[142]

All the same, wider questions remain over the strategic and operational relationship the EU and NATO should have: Will the EU continue to be viewed as appropriate only for small-scale stabilization and civilian missions, with NATO preferred for conducting high-end expeditionary operations? Or, given the EU has been at the forefront of thinking about the spectrum of tasks required for complex peace support operations and has the credibility and legitimacy that comes with its political nature, should efforts continue to enhance CSDP? Should NATO strive to enhance its own civilian capabilities—and in what ways? There remains a lack of consensus on whether a "division of labor" between NATO and the EU is desirable; while Libya demonstrated the EU's incapacity to act, over the long term a more robust defense capability allowing the EU to act independently in situations when NATO may not be willing or able to engage remains a goal that should be strived for.

It is for these reasons a new institutional structure is required to bring the U.S.-NATO-EU relationship into alignment, and U.S. leadership will be crucial for this. But despite efforts by the Obama administration to engage on this issue, the feeling remains that "The U.S. doesn't have much vision for how to make this transatlantic community vital and effective." While the United States appears to have a clear strategy for engagement with the Asia-Pacific:

> Where is the vision, the strategy, the execution in U.S. policy towards Europe? That's exactly what's missing in U.S. thinking about the transatlantic community right now.[143]

Calls for the U.S.-EU relationship to supersede that of NATO are misplaced, not least because U.S.-EU relations cannot be separated from U.S.-NATO relations. It is certainly true that the U.S.-EU relationship should continue to be strengthened and enhanced. As one expert on the transatlantic relationship has argued:

> The Americans need to reorient their relationship with the EU at a much greater strategic level, because . . . these new emerging challenges, the competencies do not lie within NATO, they lie with the EU. Cyber security, energy security, piracy, banking; what NATO's trying to do now is to develop duplicative competencies . . . it tries to do everything that it actually cannot do. What we need to do is stop investing in the duplication, and start investing in the strengthening of the US-EU relationship.[144]

An enhanced U.S.-EU partnership makes logical sense in a world where partnership and cooperation among like-minded allies are crucial in resolving transnational security threats and challenges. The framework agreement signed by Washington and Brussels in May 2011 on U.S. participation in EU crisis-management operations has been an important step in furthering such a partnership.[145] The EU's normative basis, its soft-power expertise, and greater credibility in some parts of the world ensure that it is a critical actor for the United States. Additionally, Washington has come to view CSDP as "value added," even though its operations have been modest and limited in size and often struggled with force-generation and capability shortfalls.

But enhancing the U.S.-EU partnership is only one part of fostering a revised transatlantic bargain for the 21st century. What is required is a U.S.-NATO-EU partnership, or, in the words of one commentator, a *menage a trois* between the United States, NATO, and the EU.[146] The tendency in security discourse to refer to NATO and the EU in the same breath tends to obscure the fact that these two institutions, although often operating in the same security sphere, are distinctly different. Modern security challenges invariably require a comprehensive approach; the kinds of military solutions NATO can offer will not always be appropriate and will need — as operations in the Balkans, Afghanistan, and Libya have demonstrated — multiple levers of power and a range of competencies that, in some instances, the EU will be better able to deliver. There will inevitably be some issues — climate change, Iran, counterterrorism — in which U.S.-EU relations will supersede those of U.S.-NATO; yet, U.S.-EU dialogue obviously excludes Canada and those NATO countries not members of the EU (Turkey, Norway, and Iceland). NATO, however, has an integrated military command structure and more than 60 years' experience in fostering interoperability, training, education, and exchanges between North America, Europe, and partner nations. Given the limitations of CSDP so far, NATO thus remains the primary mechanism for conducting operations. However, the likelihood is that there will be increased requirements for joint NATO-EU action; while Libya was conducted under the auspices of NATO, the EU provided critical humanitarian assistance. Anti-piracy operations off the Horn of Africa have only served to validate the critical role of the EU as a political actor, with its ability to negotiate with other governments over the seizures or transfers of pirates. In instances when it makes sense for European nations to take the lead, as in Libya, case-by-case decisionmaking will be necessary; there is no "one size fits all" solution, nor a recipe for a neat division of labor. The EU has obvious expertise in crisis management and prevention and may take the lead in such areas, with NATO increasingly looking to use its developing, but modest, civilian capability to interface with organizations like the EU.[147]

In other operations, especially those requiring higher-end warfighting or expeditionary capabilities, or in which vital U.S. national interests are at stake, NATO will likely be the lead institution—with the EU playing a supporting or complementary role. Each organization, then, has attributes the other lacks to some degree—but both have critical relationships with the United States. The degree of U.S. engagement with each will also depend on different factors; it is impossible and unwise to suggest a "model" or template for the future. As in the case of Libya, when NATO takes the lead in an operation, the United States may act in a supporting or enabling capacity; should there be future large-scale operations such as in Afghanistan, where vital U.S. national interests are at stake, the United States will undoubtedly continue to play the leading role. Yet, invariably, there will also be circumstances in which it makes sense for the EU to be the lead actor—the EU has, in many ways, greater credibility and legitimacy than the United States and NATO, especially in parts of Africa, the Middle East, and the Arab world. While Berlin Plus provides a mechanism for the EU to act using NATO's operational headquarters (HQ), there are also strong arguments in favor of a fully operational EU command-and-control capability that would allow states like the UK, France, and Germany to multinationalize their own national headquarters to conduct a CSDP operations.[148] This remains a contested issue; while

France and other EU members are in support of such a move, the UK continues to oppose it. However, an operational EU HQ should, in theory, be in Washington's interests; implementing one would allow the EU to act more quickly and robustly without recourse to Berlin Plus or the need to rely on the United States. Currently, there is some U.S.-EU military cooperation. U.S. Naval Forces Africa (NAVAF) already cooperates with a number of EU nations to coordinate maritime operations and drug and crime interdiction in Africa, while there is potential for cooperation between the U.S. African Command (AFRICOM), the European Command (EUCOM), and the EU.[149]

In short, given the nature of modern security challenges, as well as fiscal and geostrategic imperatives, gone is the day when a transatlantic division of labor between the United States and Europe might have been appropriate. What is required is greater institutional flexibility and adaptation, to generate the kind of functioning, effective, and coherent relationship necessary to foster a transatlantic bargain fit for the 21st century. As Leo Michel argues:

> NATO increasingly will need to share the stage with the EU as a security and defense actor in its own right. This means that the United States, which stands to benefit in many ways from a growing bilateral relationship with the EU, should be open to a virtuous ménage à trois.[150]

## PART IV: CONCLUSION AND RECOMMENDATIONS

When one surveys the trajectory of NATO's evolution from Bosnia to Benghazi over the past 2 decades, it is hard not to conclude that the transatlantic bargain that has underpinned the alliance—and defined America's relationship with NATO—is in urgent need of revision if it is to survive for another 60 years. As Sten Rynning has written, NATO's future rests on careful statesmanship that balances both hope and realism.[151] It is naïve to think that NATO can jettison the burden-sharing debates that have been such an integral part of its history, or pretend they can be solved by quick fixes and new concepts: they are part and parcel of what NATO is and will be an enduring feature of its future. In the words of Aldous Huxley, "The charms of history and its enigmatic lessons consist in the fact that, from age to age, nothing changes and yet everything is completely different."[152] The same may be said of the transatlantic bargain; debates over burden sharing between the United States and its European allies are as old as the alliance itself, and they will not disappear. The transatlantic bargain has always been a balancing act between a U.S. commitment to European security, in return for a position of U.S. leadership and dominance of NATO and the expectation that Europeans would accelerate efforts to provide for their own defense. Such a balance remains the essence of the bargain in the 21st century, but the context within which the bargain has to operate has changed dramatically, and the nature of America's relationship with the alliance is perhaps under more scrutiny than ever before.

In the context of the contemporary security environment, one characterized by the complexity of modern operations requiring a range of civilian and military capabilities, and a changing world characterized by the diffusion of power and the rise of China, the Atlantic Alliance—and the transatlantic bargain that underpins it—must by necessity reorient itself to this changing landscape. NATO began a process of adaptation and adjustment at the end of the Cold War, gradually restructuring and reforming to take on a core role in crisis management. However, the combined experiences of NATO's missions in the Balkans, a decade-long expeditionary operation in Afghanistan, and its most recent mission in Libya, coupled with a climate of fiscal austerity on both sides of the Atlantic, have placed the bargain under immense strain. During the first Obama administration, it became evident that Washington is becoming less and less willing to tolerate what it sees as fundamental gaps within the Alliance—in defense spending, capabilities, and military transformation. As a result, Washington is signaling more forcefully than ever to its European allies that they must take on a greater share of Alliance burdens, accelerate efforts to generate capabilities and resources, and move away from a deeply entrenched culture of dependency. Europe has a growing recognition that its relationship with America is changing—the result of a shifting geopolitical landscape that is compelling the United States to reorient its strategic focus.

A consensus has thus emerged on both sides of the Atlantic that the transatlantic bargain that has underpinned NATO for over 60 years is both outdated and unsuited to the demands of a radically different geopolitical environment from the one that gave rise to it. But the debate over the nature of the transatlantic bargain and the state of transatlantic relations in the 21st century is one partially rooted in misperceptions and insecurities that are unhelpful in framing thinking about what a revised bargain should look like. The use of the term "pivot" in framing U.S. engagement in the Asia-Pacific unhelpfully underscored notions that the United States was turning away from Europe—a perception that had already been fueled by Europe's own insecurities about its future. The U.S. tendency to berate Europeans perpetually over burden sharing has also been both unhelpful and misguided, over-simplifying a complex issue. Claims of the "pacification" or "demilitarization" of Europe do not stand up to scrutiny, but Europe's inability to emerge as a global strategic actor and generate a coherent defense capability has also given rise to the paradoxical position of the United States — both lambasting NATO for its inadequacies, while at the same time according it preference over the EU in U.S. strategic thinking. While Washington continues to berate its allies, urging European nations to "step up," it also continues to proclaim itself the "indispensible nation" within NATO — an attitude that does little to encourage a shift away from the culture of dependency that has defined the Alliance for so long. The result is a trans-atlantic bargain that has stagnated, mired in history and unsuited to the changing security environment of the 21st century.

**Beyond the Transatlantic Bargain.**

There are signs, however, that not only is there a consensus on the need to revise the transatlantic bargain, but also that outlines of what such a bargain might look like are beginning to emerge. U.S. rebalancing toward the Asia-Pacific and a reduction in U.S. forces in Europe in no way signals a turning away from Europe, only a recognition that the United States inhabits a changing world; this is a process that has essentially been under way since the end of the Cold War, but has been accelerated in the context of the challenges and demands of a decade of war, a climate of austerity, and the rise of new centers of power. U.S. political and military leaders should continue to affirm NATO's enduring importance and value for America, such as President Obama sought to do at the Chicago Summit, to offset concerns in some parts of Europe that America's commitment to the Alliance and the region may be waning, and to continue to be an engine to drive NATO's transformation. Recent speeches by Panetta have sounded a more constructive tone, reassuring allies that U.S. troop reductions in Europe do not mean a reduction in the U.S. commitment to Europe.[153]

As Panetta made clear, while the U.S. military may be reconfiguring its force posture to reflect the wider strategic rebalancing to the Asia-Pacific, the U.S. military should, and will, continue to support regular rotational deployments to conduct joint training with its European allies and to ensure that both sides are able to operate together on future missions.[154] Moreover, U.S. military rebalancing in Asia involves primarily naval assets. In this regard, the role of the U.S. Army in Europe (USAREUR), although reduced in size, will continue to play a pivotal role in building partner capacity and fostering interoperability through ongoing training and exercises with European allies. Continuing multinational Landpower exercises of the kind currently undertaken by USAREUR will be a valuable tool in demonstrating the U.S. military's ongoing commitment to capacity building and partnership in Europe. These exercises should also be part of wider, coordinated efforts to reassure Europe that, at a time of U.S. strategic flux and change, Europe remains central to U.S. strategic and military thinking.

The affirmation of America's commitment to Europe and NATO should help dispel any misperceptions or insecurities in Europe that a changing relationship with the region implies a waning commitment or turning away from the region. In return, European allies must demonstrate the maturity and leadership required to help forge a revised transatlantic bargain. To be sure, Europe has its own internal difficulties, which complicate the challenge of revising the transatlantic bargain, but at a time when multinational defense collaboration is accelerating across Europe, there are signs at least that European allies recognize and understand the importance of more efficient and coordinated efforts to generate resources and capabilities that can reduce their dependency on Washington. The United States has vital interests in seeing defense reform and collaboration accelerate and deepen across Europe, and should continue to encourage and promote effective cooperation between ACT and EDA, the drivers of defense transformation on both sides of the Atlantic. While the economic crisis and divergent views over the merits of intervening in Libya have undermined the EU's CSDP, a revised transatlantic bargain for the 21st century cannot simply be one between the United States and NATO, but must also acknowledge and reflect the growing complexity of the European security architecture.

Washington should continue to support the development of a growing strategic partnership between the EU and NATO. In particular, future U.S. leaders may well find it in the country's interests to encourage key allies such as the UK to support the establishment of an EU operational HQ to provide for a more effective and robust EU planning capability that will allow the EU to take on missions it may be more suited to handle. In short, revising the transatlantic bargain requires not only a new model of burden sharing within NATO, but a rethinking of the Berlin Plus arrangements that require the EU to outsource both the conduct and command and control of its operations to SHAPE or to a national OHQ. Washington and London have long resisted this, partly out of concern over unnecessary duplication and an undermining of the centrality of NATO. But forging a truly strategic partnership among the United States, NATO, and the EU may well require a rethinking of the relationship between these two institutions, based on a pragmatic understanding of how European security has evolved since the end of the Cold War. NATO may, at least in the short term, continue to be the primary mechanism for conducting military operations, with CSDP playing a supporting role or taking on only small-scale missions. However, the EU's growing competency in a range of issues, from climate change and terrorism, to energy security, development, and crisis management, make it a critical actor in transatlantic security affairs. The EU must, therefore, be at the center of a revised bargain.

Revising the transatlantic bargain for the 21st century is no easy task, and there are no "quick-fixes." Much ink has been spilt, books and commentaries written, and summits and meetings held over the current state of transatlantic relations and the future of NATO and Europe—and many more will follow. While there may be a broad consensus that the transatlantic bargain requires adapting and revising, the ways in which it needs to adapt, the scale of that adaptation and the willingness to implement it remain contested. That the debate has begun, however contentious and difficult, is to be applauded. NATO is an alliance that has, since its inception, shown itself to have a quite remarkable capacity for self-reflection and adaptation.

It is nothing if not resilient, and while NATO summits typically result in a barrage of platitudes, vague statements, and photo opportunities, they also reveal an alliance continually reassessing and analyzing its merits and its weaknesses, its past and future, its challenges, and opportunities. Although the future is, as ever, uncertain, the challenge facing Obama and future American Presidents is how to maintain America's commitment to NATO, while helping foster a revised — and wider — transatlantic bargain commensurate with the realities and challenges of the 21st century. Such a bargain requires a shift in thinking about European security matters on both sides of the Atlantic. Washington should resist the tendency to compartmentalize the "U.S. and NATO" and the "U.S. and EU" but endeavor to encourage a more integrated and nuanced approach to transatlantic security relations. In Europe, political will and a sounder fiscal basis are required if CSDP is to achieve its potential and the EU is to take its place at the center of a revised bargain. It remains impossible to determine how the European economic crisis will play out, but given Europe's capacity to weather previous crises and the recognition that too much has been achieved for the crisis to be undone, there is cause for hope. The United States certainly has its own domestic and fiscal challenges, but if anything, it is precisely because of these challenges that now more than ever, a new transatlantic bargain is required. The transatlantic bargain was a Cold War construct suited to its time; what is required now is a transatlantic bargain that can balance hope and realism, and generate a new culture of transatlantic partnership.

# ENDNOTES

1. Barack Obama, "A World that Stands as One," Berlin, Germany, July 24, 2008, available from *my.barackobama.com/page/community/post/obamaroadblog/gGxyd4*.

2. David S. Yost, *NATO Transformed: The Alliance's New Roles in International Security*, Washington DC: United States Institute for Peace, 1998, p. 29.

3. Stephen Chan, *The End of Certainty: Towards A New Internationalism*, New York, and London, UK: Zed Books, 2010.

4. Harlan Cleveland, *NATO: The Transatlantic Bargain*, New York: Harper & Row, 1970, p. 5.

5. Geir Lundestad, *The United States and Western Europe since 1945*, Oxford, UK: Oxford University Press, 2003, p. 50.

6. Jens Ringsmose, "Burden-Sharing Redux," *Contemporary Security Policy*, Vol. 31, No. 2, p. 321.

7. See, for example, David P. Calleo, *Follies of Power: America's Unipolar Fantasy*, Cambridge, UK: Cambridge University Press, 2009; Robert J. Lieber, "Persistent Primacy and the Future of the American Era," *International Politics*, Vol. 46, 2009, pp. 119-139; James M. Lindsay, "George W. Bush, Barack Obama and the Future of US Global Leadership," *International Affairs*, Vol. 87, No. 4, 2001, pp. 765-779; Robin Niblett, "Ready to Lead? Rethinking America's Role in a Changed World," *A Chatham House Report*, 2009, available from *www.chathamhouse.org.uk/publications/papers/view/-/id/706/*; Fareed Zakaria, *The Post-American World and the Rise of the Rest*, New York: W. W. Norton & Co., 2008.

8. See Stephen Lee Myers and Thom Shanker, "NATO Expansion, and a Bush Legacy, Are in Doubt," *The New York Times*, March 15, 2008, available from *www.nytimes.com/2008/03/15/world/europe/15nato.html?_r=1&pagewanted=all*.

9. See "Gates Demands More Troops Willing to 'Fight and Die' in Afghanistan," *The Guardian*, February 7, 2008, available from *www.guardian.co.uk/politics/2008/feb/07/foreignpolicy.uk*.

10. General James Jones, "NATO Transformation and Challenges," *RUSI Journal*, Vol. 150, No. 2, p. 15.

11. Karl-Heinz Kamp and Kurt Volker, "Toward a New Transatlantic Bargain," Washington, DC: Carnegie Endowment for International Peace, February 1, 2012, p. 5.

12. Lundestad, pp. 70-71.

13. Charles A. Cooper and Benjamin Zycher, *Perceptions of NATO Burden-Sharing*, Santa Monica, CA: The RAND Corporation, June 1989, pp. vi-viii, available from *www.rand.org/content/dam/rand/pubs/reports/2009/R3750.pdf*.

14. *The Report of the Committee of Three on Non-Military Cooperation*, NATO, 1956, available from *www.nato.int/docu/basictxt/bt-a3.htm*.

15. Karl W. Deutsch, *Political Community and the North Atlantic Area*, Princeton, NJ: Princeton University Press, 1957, p. 5.

16. Kamp and Volker, p. 5.

17. John A. Hall, "Passions within Reasons," Jeffrey Anderson, G. John Ikenberry, and Thomas Risse, eds., *The End of the West: Crisis and Change in the Atlantic Order*, Ithaca, NY, and London, UK: Cornell University Press, 2008, p. 241.

18. Kenneth Waltz, "Structural Realism after the Cold War," *International Security*, Vol. 25, No. 1, 2000, p. 21.

19. For more on this "institutional logic" argument, see G. John Ikenberry, "Institutions, Strategic Restraint and the Persistence of American Postwar Order," *International Security*, Vol. 23, No. 3, Winter 1998-99, pp. 43-78.

20. Germany provided the main base for U.S. troops in Europe. According to a report by the Heritage Foundation, during the Cold War, 250,000 troops were billeted in West Germany, but by 1993, this number had fallen to 105,254. Thousands of U.S. troops were also withdrawn from the UK after 1990, and Spain

saw a reduction from around 9,000 to 2,000. Other reductions of around 50 percent occurred in Portugal, Iceland, Greece, and the Netherlands. See Tim Kane, "Global U.S. Troop Deployment, 1950-2003," Washington, DC: The Heritage Foundation, October 27, 2004, available from *www.heritage.org/research/reports/2004/10/global-us-troop-deployment-1950-2003*.

21. Keith Hartley and Todd Sandler, "NATO Burden-Sharing: Past and Future," *Journal of Peace Research*, Vol. 3, No. 6, 1999, p. 572.

22. Ringsmose.

23. For a good analysis of contributions to this campaign, see John E. Peters, Nora Bensahel, Stuart Johnson, Timothy Liston, and Traci Williams, *European Contributions to Operation Allied Force: Implications for Transatlantic Cooperation*, Santa Monica, CA: RAND, 2001.

24. James Sperling and Mark Webber, "NATO: From Kosovo to Kabul," *International Affairs*, Vol. 85, No. 3, 2009, p. 498.

25. See Ellen Hallams, *The US and NATO Since 9/11: The Transatlantic Alliance Renewed*, Abingdon, UK: Routledge, 2010, pp. 58-59. See also Philip H. Gordon, "NATO After September 11," *Survival*, Vol. 43, No. 4, 2001; Tom Lansford, *All for One: Terrorism, NATO and the US*, Aldershot, UK: Ashgate Publishing Limited, 2002.

26. M. J. Williams, *The Good War: NATO and the Liberal Conscience in Afghanistan*, Basingstoke, UK: Palgrave MacMillan, 2011, p. 61.

27. *Ibid.*, p. 51.

28. See Tim Bird and Alex Marshall, *Afghanistan: How the West Lost Its Way*, New Haven, CT, and London, UK: Yale University Press, 2011, pp. 116-117.

29. For a detailed account of the formulation of strategy on Afghanistan, see *ibid.*

30. See M. J. Williams, *NATO, Security and Risk Management: From Kosovo to Khandahar*, Abindgon, UK: Routledge, 2008.

31. Christopher Coker, "Between Iraq and a Hard Place: Multinational Co-operation, Afghanistan and Strategic Culture," *RUSI Journal*, October 2006, Vol. 151, No.5, p. 17.

32. Ellen Hallams and Benjamin Schreer, "Towards a 'Post-American' Alliance? NATO Burden-Sharing After Libya," *International Affairs*, Vol. 88, No. 2, 2012, p. 317.

33. Bird and Marshall, pp. 154-155.

34. M. J. Williams, p. 96.

35. Ikenberry, p. 13.

36. Risse, "The End of the West," Ikenberry, Anderson, and Risse, eds., pp. 285-287.

37. Timo Noetzel and Benjamin Schreer, "Does a Multi-Tier NATO Matter? The Atlantic Alliance and the Process of Strategic Change," *International Affairs*, Vol. 85, No. 2, 2009, p. 215.

38. Barack Obama's speech to the Democratic National Convention, Denver, CO, August 28, 2008, available from *www.demconvention.com/barack-obama/*.

39. Barack Obama, "Renewing American Leadership," *Foreign Affairs*, July/August 2007.

40. Obama, "A World that Stands as One."

41. Carl Pederson, *Obama's America*, Edinburgh, Scotland: Edinburgh University Press, 2009, pp. 31-33.

42. See, for example, Martha C. Nussbaum, ed., *For Love of Country? In a New Democracy Forum on the Limits of Patriotism*, Boston, MA: Beacon Press, 2002.

43. See Jonathan Alter, *The Promise: President Obama Year One*, London, UK, and New York: Simon & Schuster, 2010, p. 226.

44. *Ibid.*, p. 225.

45. See *Strategic Survey: North America*, London, UK: International Institute of Strategic Studies, Vol. 109, No. 1, September 2009, p. 92.

46. James Lindsay, "George W. Bush, Barack Obama and the Future of U.S. Global Leadership," *International Affairs*, Vol. 87, No. 4, 2011, p. 773.

47. "George H. W. Obama?" *Foreign Policy*, April 14 2010, available from *www.foreignpolicy.com/articles/2010/04/14/george_ hw_obama*.

48. "Remarks by the President on a New Strategy for Afghanistan and Pakistan," Washington, DC: The White House, March 27, 2009, available from *www.whitehouse.gov/the_press_office/Remarks- by-the-President-on-a-New-Strategy-for-Afghanistan-and-Pakistan/*.

49. See Peter Baker, "Obama's War Over Terror," *The New York Times*, January 4, 2012, available from *www.nytimes. com/2010/01/17/magazine/17Terror-t.html?pagewanted=all&_r=0*.

50. Cited in Bob Woodward, *Obama's Wars*, New York: Simon and Schuster, 2010, p. 135.

51. See "On European Trip, President Tries to Set a New, Pragmatic Tone," *The Washington Post*, April 5, 2009, available from *www.washingtonpost.com/wpdyn/content/article/2009/04/04/ AR2009040400700.html*.

52. "Remarks by Vice President Biden at 45th Munich Conference on Security Policy," Munich, Germany, February 7, 2009, available from *www.whitehouse.gov/the_press_office/RemarksbyVice- PresidentBidenat45thMunichConferenceonSecurityPolicy/*.

53. Will Englund, "Obama's Lukewarm Start With Europe," *The National Journal*, March 13, 2010, available from *www.national- journal.com/njmagazine/nj_20100313_6226.php*.

54. "NATO Backs Obama's Afghan Plan but Pledges Few New Troops," April 5, 2009, *The Washington Post*, available from *www.washingtonpost.com/wpdyn/content/article/2009/04/04/AR2009040402594.html*.

55. See "On European Trip, President Tries to Set a New, Pragmatic Tone."

56. See "Summit Declaration on Afghanistan Issued by the Heads of State and Government Participating in the Meeting of the North Atlantic Council in Strasbourg/Kehl," April 4, 2009, available from *www.nato.int/cps/en/natolive/news_52836.htm?mode=pressrelease*.

57. See "NATO Backs Obama's Afghan Plan but Pledges Few New Troops."

58. Alter, p. 363.

59. Woodward, p. 294.

60. See James Kirkup, "Barack Obama's 'Dithering' Hurts Afghan Mission, British Sources Say," *The Telegraph*, November 5, 2009, available from *www.telegraph.co.uk/news/worldnews/asia/afghanistan/6509608/Barack-Obamas-dithering-hurts-Afghan-mission-British-sources-say.html*.

61. See Englund, "Obama's Lukewarm Start with Europe."

62. See "Europe Reluctant to Pledge More Troops," *Spiegel Online*, December 2, 2009, available from *www.spiegel.de/international/europe/0,1518,664828,00.html*.

63. See Mark Lander, "NATO Pledges 7,000 Troops, but Avoids Details," *The New York Times*, December 4, 2009, available from *www.nytimes.com/2009/12/05/world/asia/05diplo.html?hp*.

64. See Richard Auxier, "Few in NATO Support Call For Additional Forces in Afghanistan," Washington, DC: Pew Research Center, August 31, 2009, available from *pewresearch.org/pubs/1325/little-support-in-nato-for-afghanistan-troop-increases*.

65. Germany and Britain increased their troop numbers by 500, Poland by 600, and Italy by 1,000, while Georgia, Portugal, and Slovakia also pledged to increase troop numbers.

66. See Englund, "Obama's Lukewarm Start with Europe."

67. See Ian Traynor, "'Pacification' of Europe is Threat to security, U.S. tells NATO," *The Guardian*, February 23, 2010, available from *www.guardian.co.uk/world/2010/feb/23/pacification-europe-security-threat-us-nato*.

68. *Ibid.*

69. "The Security and Defense Agenda (Future of NATO)," Speech by Secretary Gates, Brussels, Belgium, June 10, 2011, available from *www.defense.gov/speeches/speech.aspx?speechid=1581*.

70. James Sperling and Mark Webber, 'NATO: From Kosovo to Kabul,' *International Affairs*, Vol. 85, No. 3, 2009, p. 503.

71. Anders Fogh Rasmussen, "Taking Stock of the Alliance," *The New York Times*, May 16, 2012, available from *www. nytimes.com/2012/05/17/opinion/taking-stock-of-the-atlantic-alliance. html?_r=1*.

72. For a robust critique of U.S. militarism, see Andrew J. Bacevich, *The New American Militarism: How Americans Are Seduced By War*, Oxford, UK: Oxford University Press, 2005.

73. *Leading Through Civilian Power: The First Quadrennial Diplomacy and Development Review*, Washington, DC: U.S. Department of State, January 2010, available from *www.state.gov/documents/organization/153108.pdf*.

74. Hans Binnendijk, "Defense Issues for the NATO Summit," Testimony before the Senate Foreign Relations Committee, May 10, 2012, p. 2, available from *www.foreign.senate.gov/imo/media/doc/Hans_Binnendijk_Testimony.pdf*.

75. See Stephen Fidler and Alistair MacDonald, "Europeans Retreat on Defense Spending," *The Wall Street Journal Europe*, April 23, 2011, available from online.*wsj.com/article/SB100014240 531119034613045765245036258299 70.html*.

76. Anand Menon, "European Defense Policy from Lisbon to Libya," *Survival*, Vol. 53, No. 3, 2011, pp. 75–90.

77. See Terry Terriff, "De ja vu all over again? September 11, 2001 and NATO Military Transformation," Ellen Hallams, Luca Ratti, and Benjamin Zyla, eds., *Beyond 9/11: The Transformation of the Atlantic Alliance*, Basingstoke, UK: Palgrave MacMillan, forthcoming, 2013.

78. This issue will be explored in greater detail in Part III.

79. In 1979, Brzezinski wrote that:

An arc of crisis stretches along the shores of the Indian Ocean, with fragile social and political structures in a region of vital importance to us threatened with fragmentation. The resulting political chaos could well be filled by elements hostile to our values and sympathetic to our adversaries.

The term took on a heightened significance for many in the West in the context of 9/11, although it is also a highly contentious one. See Michael Clarke, "The Middle East: The Growing Arc of Crisis," *The World Today*, Vol. 60, No. 11, November 2004.

80. Jeremy Shapiro and Nick Witney, *Towards a Post-American Europe: A Power Audit of US–EU Relations*, Cambridge, UK: European Council on Foreign Relations, 2009, p. 11.

81. See Daniel W. Drezner, "Does Obama Have a Grand Strategy? Why We Need Doctrines in Uncertain Times," *Foreign Affairs*, Vol. 90, No. 4, 2011, p. 58.

82. "Remarks by the President in Address to the Nation on Libya," Washington, DC: The White House, March 28, 2011, available from *www.whitehouse.gov/the-press-office/2011/03/28/remarks-president-address-nation-libya*.

83. Hallams and Schreer, "Towards a 'Post-American' Alliance? NATO Burden-Sharing after Libya," p. 321.

84. "Mr Gates's Sermon," *The Washington Post*, June 14, 2011, p. A18.

85. Ryan Lizza, "The Consequentialist: How the Arab Spring Remade Obama's Foreign Policy," *The New Yorker*, May 2, 2011, available from *www.newyorker.com/reporting/2011/05/02/110502fa_fact_lizza?currentPage=all*.

86. *Accidental Heroes: Britain, France and the Libya Operation*, London, UK: Royal United Services Institute, 2011, p. 9.

87. Binnendijk.

88. Damon M. Wilson, "Learning from Libya: The Right Lessons for NATO," Washington, DC: Atlantic Council, 2011, p. 2, available from *www.acus.org/files/publication_pdfs/403/090111_ACUS_LearningLibya_Wilson*.

89. Author interview, senior U.S. official, U.S. Mission to NATO, NATO HQ, Brussels, Belgium, October 27, 2011.

90. Stephane Abrial, "NATO in a Time of Austerity," *The New York Times*, May 17, 2012, available from *www.nytimes.com/2012/05/18/opinion/nato-in-a-time-of-austerity.html?_r=1*.

91. "The Security and Defense Agenda (Future of NATO)," Speech by Secretary Gates.

92. U.S. Defense Budget: Priorities and Choices, Washington, DC: U.S. Department of Defense, January 2012, available from *www.defense.gov/news/Defense_Budget_Priorities.pdf*.

93. Author interview, U.S. Representative, House Armed Services Committee, Washington, DC, June 15, 2011.

94. Stephen J. Coonan, "The Widening Military Capabilities Gap between the United States and Europe: Does it Matter?" *Parameters*, Autumn 2006, pp. 75-76.

95. S. 2177: NATO Enhancement Act of 2012, March 8, 2012, available from *www.lugar.senate.gov/news/record.cfm?id=336260*.

96. As of December 31, 2011, this figure stood at approximately 22 percent. See "NATO Common-funded Budgets and Programmes: Cost Share Arrangements Valid from 1/1/2010 to 31/12/2011," available from *www.nato.int/nato_static/assets/pdf/pdf_2010_01/20101102_NATO_common_funded_budgets_2010-2011.pdf*.

97. Cited in Ringsmose.

98. Cited in Daniel Hamilton, ed., *Transatlantic Transformations: Equipping NATO for the 21st Century*, Washington, DC: Center for Transatlantic Relations, 2004, p. 5.

99. Timothy Edmunds, "The Defence Dilemma in Britain," *International Affairs*, Vol. 86, No. 2, 2010, p. 380.

100. Speech by General James Mattis, Supreme Allied Commander Transformation, "A Transformation Perspective," *Launching NATO's New Strategic Concept*, Brussels, Belgium, July 9, 2009, available from *www.nato.int/cps/en/natolive/opinions_56392.htm*.

101. For a more detailed analysis of NATO's transformation process, see Terry Terriff, Frans Osinga, and Theo Farrell, eds., *A Transformation Gap? American Innovations and European Military Change*, Stanford, CA: Stanford University Press, 2010.

102. Cited in Jorge Benitez, "NATO Allies Grapple with Shrinking Defense Budgets," Washington, DC: Atlantic Council, January 30, 2012, available from *www.acus.org/natosource/nato-allies-grapple-shrinking-defense-budgets*.

103. Thomas Ries, "The Lost Alliance: NATO in Chicago," Washington, DC: Atlantic Council, May 22, 2012, available from *www.acus.org/new_atlanticist/lost-alliance-nato-chicago*.

104. "The Security and Defense Agenda (Future of NATO)."

105. See, for example, Hallams and Schreer, "Towards a 'Post-American' Alliance?"; Kamp, "The Transatlantic Link Beyond Chicago," Rome, Italy, NATO Defence College Research Reports, May 2012; Barry Pavel and Jeff Lightfoot, "The Transatlantic Bargain After the Pivot," *Atlantic Council Issue Brief*, May 22, 2012,

available from *www.acus.org/publication/transatlantic-bargain-after-pivot*; Shapiro and Witney, *Towards a Post-American Europe*; Jamie Shea, "Keeping NATO Relevant," Washington, DC: Carnegie Endowment for International Peace, April 2012, available from *www.carnegieendowment.org/2012/04/19/keeping-nato-relevant/acl9*; Stanley Sloan, *NATO, the European Union and the Atlantic Community: The Transatlantic Bargain Reconsidered*, Lanham, MD: Rowman & Littlefield Publishers Inc.; Stanley Sloan, *Permanent Alliance? NATO and the Transatlantic Bargain from Truman to Obama*, New York: Continuum Books, 2010.

106. Cleveland, pp. 5-6.

107. Author interview, senior U.S. official, U.S. Mission to NATO, NATO HQ, Brussels, October 27, 2011.

108. Jeffrey H. Michaels, "NATO After Libya," *RUSI Journal*, Vol. 65, No. 6, December 2012, p. 58.

109. Ian Bzrezinski, "Senate Testimony on NATO: Chicago and Beyond," Washington, DC: Atlantic Council, May 10, 2012, available from *www.acus.org/news/ian-brzezinski-senate-testimony-nato-chicago-and-beyond*.

110. Testimony by Wilson, U.S. House of Representatives Committee on Foreign Affairs, Subcommittee on Europe and Eurasia Hearing, "NATO: The Chicago Summit and U.S. Policy," April 26, 2012, available from *foreignaffairs.house.gov/112/HHRG-112-FA14-WState-WilsonD-20120426.pdf*.

111. Shapiro and Witney, p. 14.

112. Henry R. Luce, "The American Century," *LIFE magazine,* February 17, 1941, available from *www.informationclearinghoU.S.e.info/article6139.htm*.

113. Pavel and Lightfoot.

114. See Sten Rynning, *NATO in Afghanistan: The Liberal Disconnect*, Stanford, CA: Stanford University Press, California, 2012, p. 18.

115. Alexander Mattelaer, "How Afghanistan Has Strengthened NATO," *Survival*, December/January 2012.

116. Author interview, NATO official, Allied Command Transformation, Norfolk, VA, June 7, 2011.

117. Schreer, "Beyond Afghanistan: NATO's Partnerships in the Asia Pacific," NATO Defence College Research Paper No. 75, Rome, Italy: NATO Defence College, April 2012, p. 1.

118. For a detailed analysis on NATO's partnerships with the MENA region, see Florence Gaub, *Against All Odds: Relations with the MENA Region*, Carlisle, PA: Strategic Studies Institute, U.S. Army War College, August 2012.

119. John Barry, "The U.S.-EU-NATO Relationship—Addressing 21st Century Challenges," Florence, Italy: The European Institute, February 2012, available from *www.europeaninstitute. org/EA-February-2012/the-us-eu-nato-relationship-addressing-21st-century-challenges.html*.

120. See Sven Biscop, "NATO, ESDP, and the Riga Summit: No Transformation without Re-Equilibration," *Egmont Paper 11*, Brussels, Belgium: Royal Institute for International Affairs, May 2006.

121. *Ibid.*, pp. 8-9.

122. Author interview, NATO official, Allied Command Transformation, Norfolk, VA, June 7, 2011. See also Barry, "The U.S.-EU-NATO Relationship."

123. Cited in Sarwar Kashmeri, *NATO 2.0: Reboot or Delete?* Washington, DC: Potomac Books, 2011, p. 89.

124. Author interview, U.S. official, Washington DC, June 10, 2011.

125. *Sustaining U.S. Global Leadership*, p. 3.

126. *Ibid.*

127. Author interview, U.S. official, Washington, DC, June 10, 2011.

128. Author interview, James Goldgeier, Washington, DC, June 6, 2011.

129. Author interview, U.S. official, Washington, DC, June 10, 2011.

130. "Summit Declaration on Defence Capabilities: Toward NATO Forces 2020," Press Release 064, May 20, 2012, available from *www.nato.int/cps/en/natolive/official_texts_87594.htm?mode=pressrelease*.

131. Bastian Giegerich, "NATO's Smart Defence: Who's Buying?" *Survival: Global Politics and Strategy*, Vol. 54, No. 3, June-July 2012, pp. 69-77.

132. Leon Panetta, *From Tripoli to Chicago: Charting NATO's Future On The Way To The 2012 Summit*, Washington, DC: Carnegie Endowment for International Peace, October 5, 2011, available from *www.carnegieendowment.org/files/05-10 2011__Leon_Panetta_from_Tripoli_to_Chicago.pdf*.

133. Press Release 064.

134. "Summit Declaration on Defence Capabilities: Toward NATO Forces 2020."

135. Edgar Buckley and Nancy DeViney, "Change Management and Cultural Transformation in NATO: Lessons from the Public and Private Sectors," *Atlantic Council Issue Brief*, Washington, DC: Atlantic Council, May 14, 2012, available from *www.acus.org/files/publication_pdfs/403/NATOSmarter_IBM2_Cultural2.pdf*.

136. Leo Michel, "Smart Defense not a Trojan Horse," Washington, DC: Atlantic Council, September 28, 2012, available from *www.acus.org/new_atlanticist/smart-defense-not-trojan-horse*.

137. *A Diminishing Transatlantic Partnership? The Impact of the Financial Crisis on European Defense and Foreign Assistance Capabilities*, Washington, DC: Center for Strategic and International Studies (CSIS), May 2011, p. 39.

138. Author interview, Senior ACT official, Norfolk, VA, June 7, 2011.

139. Paddy Ashdown, "Europe's Free Ride on the Back of NATO Is Over," *The Daily Telegraph*, November 1, 2011.

140. *Ibid.*

141. See Leo G. Michel, "NATO, the European Union, and the United States: Why Not a Virtuous Ménage à Trois?" Washington, DC: Administrative Conference of the United States, available from *www.acus.org/files/ISP/michel_eucomib.pdf*.

142. *Ibid.*

143. See Barry, "The U.S.-EU-NATO Relationship."

144. Author interview with Heather Conley, Washington, DC, Center for Strategic and International Studies, June 9, 2011.

145. Available from *eur-lex.europa.eu/LexUriServ/LexUriServ.do?uri=OJ:L:2011:143:0002:0005:EN:PDF*.

146. Michel, "NATO, the European Union, and the United States."

147. See "Lisbon Summit Declaration," November, 2010, available from *www.nato.int/cps/en/natolive/official_texts_68828.htm*.

148. See Sven Biscop and Jo Coelment, "Europe Deploys Towards a Civil-Military Strategy for CSDP," Egmont Paper No. 49, Brussels, Belgium: Royal Institute for International Affairs, June 2011.

149. Michel, "NATO, the European Union, and the United States."

150. *Ibid.*

151. Sten Rynning, *NATO in Afghanistan: The Liberal Disconnect*, Stanford, CA: Stanford University Press, 2012, p.11.

152. Cited in Ringsmose, p. 319.

153. See David Alexander, "Panetta Calls for More Agile NATO with Wider Strategic Focus," *Reuters*, January 18, 2013, available from *ca.news.yahoo.com/panetta-calls-more-agile-nato-wider-strategic-focus-185421433.html*.

154. *Ibid.*